Planning the Office Landscape

Alvin E. Palmer

M. Susan Lewis

McGraw-Hill Book Company

New York   St. Louis   San Francisco   Auckland
Bogotá   Düsseldorf   Johannesburg   London
Madrid   Mexico   Montreal   New Delhi
Panama   São Paulo   Singapore
Sydney   Tokyo   Toronto

Library of Congress Cataloging in Publication Data

Palmer, Alvin E, date.
    Planning the office landscape.

    Bibliography: p.
    Includes indexes.
    1. Office layout.   2. Environmental engineering
(Buildings)   I. Lewis, M. Susan, date. joint author.
II. Title.
HF5547.P285   651   76-16807
ISBN 0-07-048415-5

19914   ⌐✓

1234567890   VHVH   786543210987

*The editors for this book were Jeremy Robinson and Gretlyn K. Blau,
the designer was Naomi Auerbach, and the production supervisor
was Teresa F. Leaden. It was set in VIP Souvenir
by Progressive Typographers.*

Printed and bound by Von Hoffmann Press, Inc.

For Kirby Keahey and Ray Ogden

Contents

Introduction

To many people, *office landscaping* is a familiar term; to most, it means an office space with an irregular placement of desks, an abundance of growing plants, carpeted floors, and no interior walls. Although this image may result from the office landscape concept, open offices and office landscaped spaces are not necessarily the same.

The office landscape concept is an *approach* to office planning. It precludes preconceived solutions; it is not a formula; it is an approach.

COMPLEXITY

The office landscape concept encompasses all the organization's elements and their interrelationships. This is possible because offices, whether research, publishing, insurance, etc., are basically similar in that each is a sociotechnical system consisting of people, and technical and material resources. Their similarities fall into several fundamental categories: products, procedures, social relationships, and environment and equipment.

All these categories or elements are interdependent. If one element is altered, all are affected. An extreme example would be to alter the products of an insurance office to those of a research group. Obviously, procedures, relationships, and equipment would also be affected.

The office landscape concept considers the interdependencies of these elements; and the approach, simply stated, is to plan for all the elements simultaneously. No one discipline, much less one person, is capable of or qualified for dealing with these basic elements and the ramifications of their interrelationships. Concurrent, interdisciplinary office planning is called for. The office landscape approach provides this through interdisciplinary, participatory team planning.

MISUNDERSTANDINGS

The office landscape concept is a relatively new approach to office planning. Consequently, there is a general lack of knowledge about it, both conceptually and specifically. Many architects, designers, and managers plan open offices which do not succeed because they are based on inadequate or fallacious understandings of the concept.

There is a common misunderstanding that the office landscape concept is merely a variation of a conventional approach to office planning and design. This is not true, if only because the landscape concept considers all elements of the office simultaneously, not sequentially as does the traditional approach.

Another prevalent idea is that open planning and the landscape concept are synonymous. This is true only if the landscape planning indicates that an open space is a feasible solution for a given office. Even here, the similarities are only visual—cosmetic if you like—for the preconceived open-plan office primarily considers physical environment, while the landscape concept tries to resolve and improve all the complex interrelationships of the office and the office user. If interoffice communication is requisite, and if the social and procedural relationships are dynamic, the office landscape approach may dictate an open-plan office. However, if the organizational relationships are relatively static, more conventional office solutions could be required.

There is also a general feeling that individual status and privacy are compromised by the office landscape concept. While status may be expressed differently, especially if the landscape is an open office, it does not need to be compromised if understood and planned for.

Privacy is visual and acoustical separation. By measurement, the visual and acoustical separation achieved in open offices is equal to or greater than that of comparable closed offices. For the most part, it is not a lack of actual privacy which presents problems for the open-plan user, but rather an initial feeling that privacy does not exist. When the office users participate in the planning of office landscapes, potential problems such as status and privacy are discussed early and in depth, and seldom constitute problems after move-in.

Other misunderstandings about the office landscape concept, notions based more on tradition or lack of knowledge than on fact, are discussed throughout the book.

AUDIENCE

In the past, learning about the office landscape concept meant participating in the planning of an actual landscape project, attending an appropriate conference or workshop, or piecing together and studying the few articles and papers written on the subject. This book is intended to make the concept more accessible, and to provide planners and users with a more complete understanding of the office landscape approach.

Users are the people who work in landscape offices; planners are those who plan, design, implement, and manage landscape projects. In the context of this book, and the office landscape concept in general, planners incorporate a large group of disciplines, including office managers and management consultants; designers, architects, and engineers; business administrators; sociologists and industrial psychologists; and furniture, equipment, and building products manufacturers. This book is written for the students and professionals of these disciplines.

PRESENTATION

Throughout the book, *text amplifiers* are used to illustrate and clarify points of emphasis. *Illustrations,* text amplifiers in graphic form, run parallel to the main body of text; and *notes,* many of which are examples from personal planning experience, are contained within the text.

Photographs of existing office landscape installations are purposely excluded because there is a tendency for first-time planners and users of the office landscape concept to imitate the existing. It is hoped that the text amplifiers will emphasize and aid the understanding of an approach, not a ready-made solution.

Costs and *acoustics* are discussed conceptually rather than specifically. It does not seem appropriate to bore the reader with detailed cost information, already outdated by current market changes. Nor does it seem appropriate to present the reader with complex acoustical jargon and formulas when principles of acoustics are more in keeping with the approach concept of the book. For these reasons, conceptual information related to both costs and acoustics appears in the book wherever appropriate.

The fundamentals of the office landscape approach are presented here in a logical sequence, but it is very important for the reader to realize from the outset that many of these are concurrent during the planning of an office landscape project.

LIMITATIONS

The office landscape concept is a valid planning approach for schools, hospitals, libraries, museums, banks, towns, etc., as well as for offices. However, this book is primarily directed toward office planning. This, in itself, is task enough.

ACKNOWLEDGMENTS

For the many pleasant hours of working with and talking over the office landscape concept, I would like to thank the following:

Fred Bach, Dieter Jaeger, Werner Lindlhar, Rod Planas, Claus Stang, and Earhard Weisner of the Quickborner Team;

Jim Cayton, Dave Hyman, and Jim Smith of LouverDrape Inc.;

Jordon Berman, Bill Brown, Wolf Geisberg, Bob Park, Lane Riland, Bob Sorensen, Jim Sulewsky, Bob Vrancken, Bill Warren, Bob Walters, Frank Carberry, and the other members of the Administrative Management Society's Office Landscape Users Group;

Parker Hirtle of Bolt Beranek and Newman;

Skip Sagar of Designcraft;

The participants of the numerous seminars and symposiums in which I was a speaker;

The managers, users, and team members of the many projects with which I have been associated; and

Especially my dear friends Herm Vande-Riet, Bob Lindblom, Don Klooster, and Len Straayer of Rose Manufacturing Company.

Alvin E. Palmer
M. Susan Lewis

Section One

Office
Landscape
History

The *office landscape concept* is an approach to office planning. The concept simultaneously considers the interrelationships of all office elements, including requirements for facile and rapid communication, optimum flexibility for arrangement and rearrangement of individual and group workplaces, and better environmental conditions.

BÜROLANDSCHAFT

Office landscape is a direct translation of the German *Bürolandschaft,* a title given the concept by journalists impressed with the genial colors, substantial number of growing plants, and openness of the first European installation. Even though the journalists' impressions seem to have been limited to the visual aspects of the concept, their title is more fitting than its English translation. *Landscape* connotes a vista or view in which the observer does not participate; *Landschaft,* on the other hand, indicates participation by the observer in the total scene. But, in spite of their inadequate descriptions of the concept, both office landscape and *Bürolandschaft* have survived more than ten years of usage.

The office landscape concept is too often associated with the open-plan office. While landscape planning may produce an open-plan solution, it is by no means interchangeable with open planning. The two came about more or less separately; the open-plan office emerged gradually from the traditional office, and the landscape concept was developed systematically by a small group of people.

The office, as we know it today, has a history of approximately one hundred years. Initially, it was a one-person space without telephone, typewriter, dictation equipment, or the other accouterments associated with the contemporary office. As industrialization spread, the office grew by increasing staff and administrative structure. Its evolution has included many phases.

The *bullpen* concept placed the staff in open spaces with rigid grids of desks and aisles. The executives were segregated to one or more sides in enclosed, windowed offices. The *single office* concept placed the staff in one, two, or more person offices. Again, the

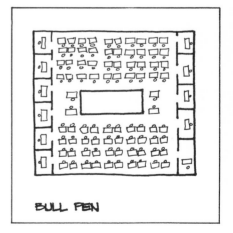

BULL PEN

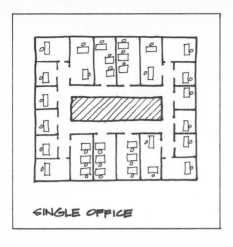

SINGLE OFFICE

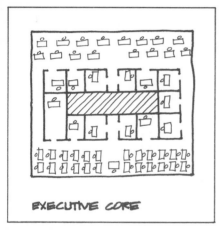

EXECUTIVE CORE

OPEN PLAN

executives were located around the building exterior in spaces with windows. Variations and combinations of the bullpen and single office—always with the executives on the outside in windowed offices—were used until the late 1950s or early 1960s, when the *executive core* concept took form. In this case, the staff was placed around the building exterior, still in open, bullpen type layouts, and the executives moved their individual offices to the building core. The executive core concept was intended to shift some of the status away from the executives and therefore reduce the growing turnover in staff-level personnel. And the executives did give up their windows, but little else.

Just how the *open office* concept emerged from these earlier plans is unclear, though the growing cost of constructing and moving office partitions undoubtedly played a part. And there is no doubt that the open office concept was a major step in the history of the office, for it was the first time both staff and executives were placed in the open, in offices of similar quality. But, once again, the executives clung to the windows.

The window has consistently been a prime factor in office design. The number of windows in a person's office has signified the importance, or status, of that individual within the organization. Even when the windows were relinquished in the executive core concept, a kind of reverse status asserted itself.

Within the last quarter century, office workers have increased phenomenally, both in number and in percentage of the total working population. At the same time, the complexion of the office has also changed. As routine office functions have become more automated, the office staff has become essentially a middle-management and executive group with a decreasing staff of clerical workers. Today, few members of these groups work individually; instead, most work in frequently changing teams and work groups. These smaller units need flexibility, individual accommodation, effective flow of communication, and the physical conditions for close teamwork.

These dynamics have caused further changes in the office: one change is the use of modular furniture, which can be arranged or added to easily; another is modular buildings, which can accommodate a variety of office sizes with relocatable partitions. Both modular systems are designed to aid in achieving flexibility.

QUICKBORNER TEAM

The Quickborner Team, a planning and management consulting firm in Germany, developed the office landscape concept in 1959. Until that time, the Quickborner Team was a materials company specializing in paper and related products, furniture and equipment, and filing systems for offices. It was out of frustration—frustration caused by a lack of harmony between products and systems—that the Quickborner Team began to investigate interdependencies within the office. This led to the realization that all elements of the office are interrelated and should be dealt with concurrently; and this, in turn, led to the development of an approach to office planning, later to be called *office landscaping.*

The first installation was in 1960, for the Bertelsman Publishing Company in Gütersloh, West Germany. Shortly thereafter, installations followed for other companies in Germany, such as Krupp, Ford, Deckel, Osram, Boehringer, Ninoflex, and Orenstein & Koppel.

In the early sixties, the concept was carried to other European countries. Office landscape projects have been completed in Spain, the Netherlands, Scandinavia, and the British Isles. Many of these projects have been occupied for several years, and today, other firms, as well as the Quickborner Team, plan and design office landscapes.

In the fall of 1967, Du Pont's Freon Products Division in Wilmington, Delaware, moved into the first office landscape space outside Europe. At about the same time, an office landscape symposium was held in Chicago. This was also the first outside Europe.

Many office landscapes throughout the United States and Canada are now several years old, and many other projects are in the planning or final design and installation stages; and interest in the office landscape concept has spread worldwide—to Australia, Africa, Asia, and Central and South America.

THE FIRST OFFICE LANDSCAPE WAS IN GÜTERSLOH, WEST GERMANY IN 1960

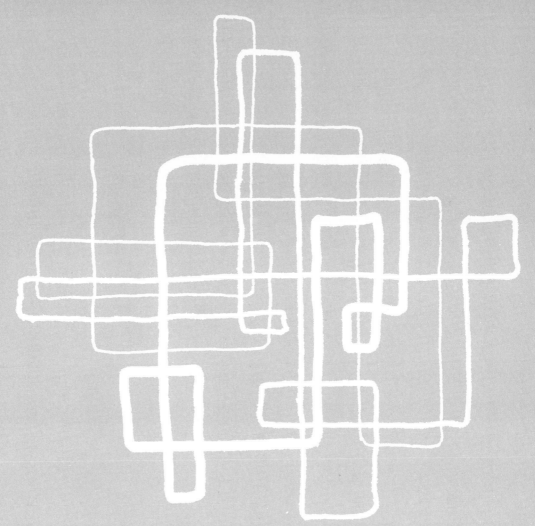

Section Two

Complexity
of
Planning

Normally, planning is thought of as the initial act or process of making plans. However, within the context of office landscaping, planning becomes cyclic, and its definition is expanded to include *developmental planning, design, implementation,* and *follow-up,* which then ties back into developmental planning, etc. Essentially, this book deals with the first planning cycle, but it is important to understand that, in order to respond to the constant changes typical of organizations, the overall planning is continuous, though the scale may be reduced considerably after the initial cycle.

The first phase of office landscaping, developmental planning, sets the direction for the given project, and specifically includes the mutual determination of goals, strategies, and priorities. Design is the bulk of the planning, involving analysis and understanding of the organization and formulation of both the means of finding new, viable solutions, and the solutions themselves. Implementation is the practical application of these solutions, and follow-up entails the testing and adjusting necessary to maintain them.

NOTE: *The developmental planning phase is crucial. Mutual determination means the establishment of goals, strategies, and priorities by all persons responsible. Too often these are set by a single high-ranking officer within the organization and never challenged, or at best, challenged too late. Priorities involve time and money and are therefore critical. It is not uncommon for a planning project to be turned upside down because a high-ranking priority setter was not aware that the lease for existing space was about to terminate, or that a new product and/or department was to be added in the near future.*

PLANNING PURPOSE

Any given system consists of elements and the relationships between these elements. In the analysis of an organization, the most important elements are people, and technical and material resources; hence, the name *sociotechnical system.* The way in which the elements of the sociotechnical system or organization are defined specifically is largely dependent on which aspect of the system is being analyzed. There are at least four

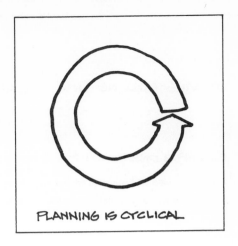

PLANNING IS CYCLICAL

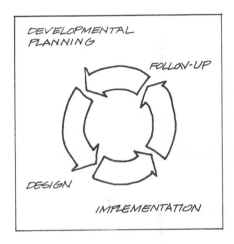

DEVELOPMENTAL PLANNING

FOLLOW-UP

DESIGN

IMPLEMENTATION

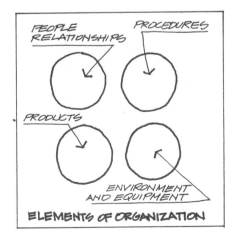

PEOPLE RELATIONSHIPS

PROCEDURES

PRODUCTS

ENVIRONMENT AND EQUIPMENT

ELEMENTS OF ORGANIZATION

DERIVING BUILDING LIFE DOLLARS

EXAMPLE ONE / OWNED BUILDING

500 EMPLOYEES @ $10,000 AVERAGE PER YEAR FOR 20 YRS. = $100,000,000	90.1% SALARIES
500 EMPLOYEES @ 200 SQ. FT. AVERAGE @ $30 PER SQ. FT. = $3,000,000 $111,000,000	2.7% BUILDING
100,000 SQ. FT. @ $4 PER SQ. FT. PER YEAR FOR 20 YRS. = $8,000,000	7.2% MAINTENANCE

EXAMPLE TWO / OWNED BUILDING

250 EMPLOYEES @ $12,500 AVERAGE PER YEAR FOR 15 YRS. = $46,875,000	90.4% SALARIES
250 EMPLOYEES @ 175 SQ. FT. AVERAGE @ $40 PER SQ. FT. = $1,750,000 $51,906,250	3.3% BUILDING
43,750 SQ. FT. @ $5 PER SQ. FT. PER YEAR FOR 15 YRS. = $3,281,250	6.3% MAINTENANCE

EXAMPLE THREE / OWNED BUILDING / FILL IN THE BLANKS

____ EMPLOYEES @ $____ AVERAGE PER YEAR FOR ___ YRS. = $_____	___ % SALARIES
____ EMPLOYEES @ _____ SQ. FT. AVERAGE @ $____ PER SQ. FT. = $_____ $_____	___ % BUILDING
____ SQ. FT. @ $_____ PER SQ. FT. PER YEAR FOR ___ YRS. = $_____	___ % MAINTENANCE

EXAMPLE FOUR / LEASED BUILDING

125 EMPLOYEES @ $15,000 AVERAGE PER YEAR FOR 10 YRS. = $18,750,000	92.0% SALARIES
125 EMPLOYEES @ 150 SQ. FT. AVERAGE @ $15 PER SQ. FT. IMPROVEMENT = $281,250 $20,437,500	1.3% BUILDING
18,750 SQ. FT. @ $7.50 PER SQ. FT. PER YEAR FOR 10 YRS. = $1,406,250	6.7% MAINTENANCE

EXAMPLE FIVE / LEASED BUILDING / FILL IN THE BLANKS

_____ EMPLOYEES @ $_____ AVERAGE PER YEAR FOR ___ YRS. = $_____	___ % SALARIES
_____ EMPLOYEES @ _____ SQ. FT. AVERAGE @ $____ PER SQ. FT. IMPROVEMENT = $_____ $_____	___ % BUILDING
_____ SQ. FT. @ $_____ PER SQ. FT. PER YEAR FOR ___ YRS. = $_____	___ % MAINTENANCE

major takeoff points within each organization: *products, procedures, people relationships,* and *environment and equipment.*

Every organization, whether considered in terms of individual departments or as a whole, exists for a purpose. This purpose is its product or products. In an industrial enterprise, the primary products may be the manufacture of a commodity and the maximization of profits, but a single department may principally produce new commodity markets.

Within the organization, there are procedures, established work steps, for obtaining specific products. These are performed by the organization's members, consequently forming people relationships within the framework of product and procedures.

The fourth element, environment and equipment, is obvious. The organization must be housed and its people must be furnished with equipment to perform their tasks.

Each of these four elements depends on, affects, and is affected by the other three. Comprehensive office planning, then, must analyze and respond to these influences and interdependencies.

Successful planning must also respond to the concurrent, interdisciplinary nature of the organization's four basic elements by considering these elements and their related disciplines simultaneously. Such planning is not simply a problem of aesthetics, and should not be approached primarily as a visual design project. It is basically a problem in work organization, whose solutions, once reached, may be implemented in any design vocabulary appropriate. Nor can office planning view organizational change as a matter of chance. In the past, change could be ignored for a generation or digested in small steps. Today, it is a dominating reality, occurring as fast as it can be measured. Planning must foresee social, technological, and economic change as fully as possible; the evolution of the office in these areas must become a conscious one. It must be understood, predicted, implemented—in short, planned.

BUILDING-LIFE DOLLARS

The importance of comprehensive planning is illustrated by a look at traditional planning in relation to

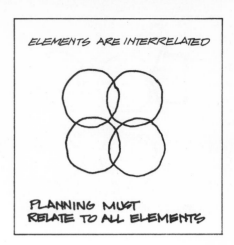

ELEMENTS ARE INTERRELATED

PLANNING MUST RELATE TO ALL ELEMENTS

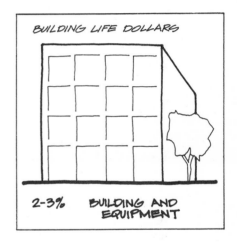

BUILDING LIFE DOLLARS

2-3%   BUILDING AND EQUIPMENT

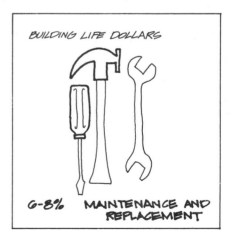

BUILDING LIFE DOLLARS

6-8%   MAINTENANCE AND REPLACEMENT

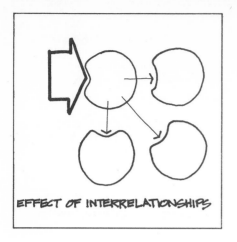

EFFECT OF INTERRELATIONSHIPS

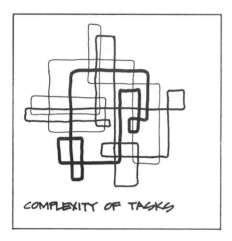

COMPLEXITY OF TASKS

BUILDING LIFE DOLLARS

90-92% SALARIES AND BENEFITS

dollars spent over the life of a building. Typically, the genesis of office planning is an organizational problem: maybe a decline in profits, a need for additional space, a desire for a better public image, or a need for bringing fragmented departments together. And typically, the organization tries to tackle its problem by concentrating on the space or building, the environment and equipment. This is the traditional approach, and, more often than not, it resolves only the symptoms of the original difficulty. The limitations of this approach become apparent through a simple review of where the organization's money goes. It may even become evident that the traditional approach directly conflicts with the organization's real needs. For example, generally only 2 to 3 percent of the total dollar outlay over the life of a building is spent on equipment and the building itself, 6 to 8 percent on maintenance and replacement, and 90 to 92 percent is spent on personnel salaries and benefits.

The point emerging clearly from these figures is that if office planning can provide more efficient operation through better communication, work and paper flow, and a resulting increase in the speed of decision making, then chances are good that total building-life costs can be reduced. This is another important factor in opting for comprehensive planning, planning which responds to and resolves all the complex interrelationships of the organization's elements.

NOTE: *The percentages above are derived from the accompanying illustration. Even if the data are altered drastically, the results still indicate that office planning, at least from a long-range economic point of view, should consider more than merely the environment and equipment.*

CONCURRENT PLANNING

Traditionally, office planning has dealt with the interrelated elements of the organization in a sequential manner. Management consultants have dealt with organizational and procedural problems, architects with siting and building considerations, interior designers with furniture and furnishings, industrial psychologists or sociologists—and in many cases, labor relations representatives—with people relationships, graphic designers with the organization's image, and so forth. Even when these different disciplines have worked simultaneously with the same organization, they usually have worked separately, with little, if any, contact. Because of the complex interdependencies of the organization's elements, this traditional approach has produced conflicting, unrelated, and limiting results.

The office landscape approach is concurrent and interdisciplinary in its consideration of organizational interrelationships. The approach itself, then, reflects the complexity of the given organization, and is accomplished through an interdisciplinary, participatory *planning team:* interdisciplinary, in that the team is composed of consultants/representatives of all the disciplines involved; and participatory, in that it involves the user. Teamwork is not a new idea in planning projects; however, in many cases, team members have come from only one discipline, and brought with them similar objectives, backgrounds, and approaches to problem solving. The office landscape planning team is not monodisciplined but multidisciplined.

PLANNING TEAM

An office landscape planning team can be organized or structured on many models of varying sizes. However, the structure should always ensure the following: involvement of representatives of all necessary disciplines, involvement of all users and if possible all future users, education and involvement of those representatives of the organization who will be responsible for follow-up planning, and no fixed leadership.

NOTE: *Many first-time office landscape planners challenge the concept of no fixed leadership, misunderstanding it to mean no leader or leadership at all. In fact, no fixed leadership simply means that the leadership changes as the major tasks and disciplines involved change.*

A team, by definition, is a number of people associated in a cooperative, coordinated effort to achieve a common aim. In order to be realistic in terms of time and economy, and to systematize the input needed for comprehensive solutions, the interdisciplinary planning team is divided into several parts. Each of these

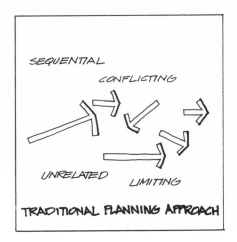

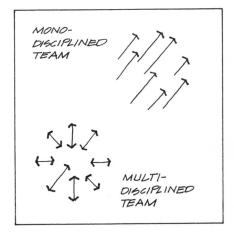

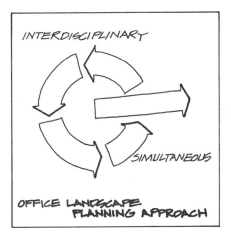

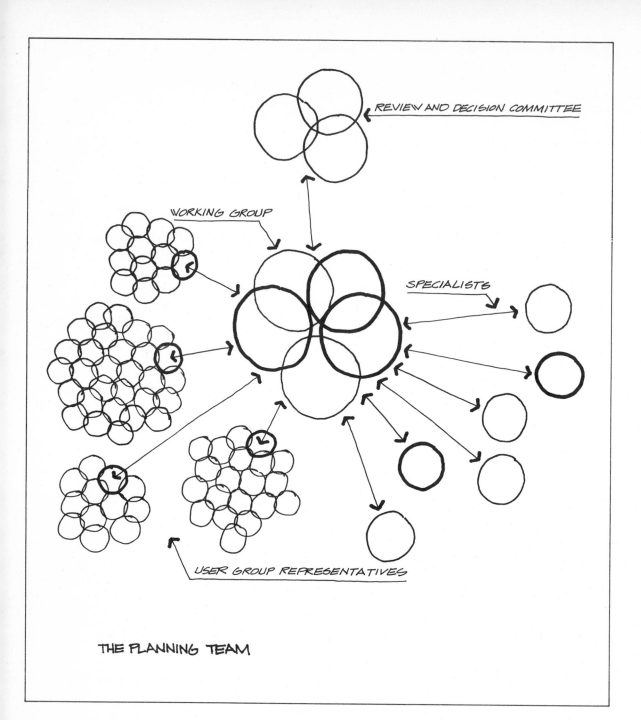

REVIEW AND DECISION COMMITTEE

WORKING GROUP

SPECIALISTS

USER GROUP REPRESENTATIVES

THE PLANNING TEAM

parts is integral to the whole, but performs specific tasks appropriate to its own makeup. In this way, every team member can be involved in depth with the information and tasks consistent with his or her discipline and/or interest, yet participate generally in all aspects of the planning.

One part of the planning team is the *working group,* which consists of approximately five persons involved full time. This is the group ultimately responsible for accomplishing the planning tasks. Working group membership can vary between three and seven; however, five is ideal for maximum communication and involvement.

The working group normally includes one person experienced in the office landscape approach; another person totally familiar with the existing inner workings of the organization, and having immediate access to its people; one person able to assist the group as receptionist, clerk, typist, etc.; and one or two other members of the organization, preferably with general planning experience. Usually, the first team member is an outside consultant and the second is a representative from the organization's middle or upper management. The third person, as a full-time member of the team, must assume more initiative and responsibility in his/her involvement in planning tasks than this stereotyped role may suggest. The selection of the last two persons is critical, for they will be responsible for the ongoing follow-up necessary to total planning.

NOTE: *Full-time team members who are also members of the organization generally devote three or four days a week to the tasks of the working group, leaving one or two days for their regular tasks. Obviously, the organization must compensate for the time given to planning by reducing normal task loads. However, it is important for working group members to maintain contact, involvement, and communication with their own departments.*

In addition to the full-time working group, the planning team includes *specialists,* who may be outside consultants or in-house professionals, each expert in a particular discipline. The specialists' involvement is sporadic, dictated by the planning tasks at hand. Normally, this group includes people knowledgeable in such disciplines or fields as architecture, interior de-

TEAM LEADERSHIP CHANGES WITH TASKS

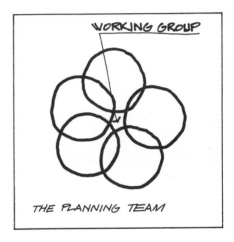

WORKING GROUP

THE PLANNING TEAM

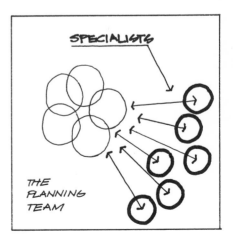

SPECIALISTS

THE PLANNING TEAM

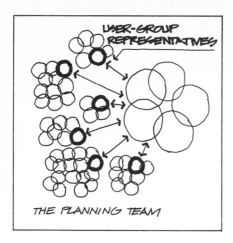

THE PLANNING TEAM

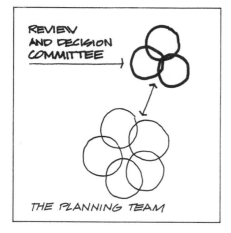

THE PLANNING TEAM

sign, acoustical engineering, sociology, furniture and equipment manufacturing, construction contracting, etc.

The third component of the planning team is the *user group,* composed of representatives of the organization's departmental subelements. Each member of this group is a liaison between the team and the users, and represents about twenty persons. The user group functions as a sounding board, providing information and criticism, both positive and negative, to aid the working group in formulating viable solutions. The user group meets with the working group as required—usually once or twice a month.

The office landscape planning team also includes a *review and decision committee,* whose function is to review and familiarize itself with planning activities and progress, and to render and/or endorse decisions as necessary. It consists of management personnel from as high a level in the organization as possible. Ideally, the review and decision committee meets with the working group at scheduled intervals of two or three weeks.

The structure of the planning team, as a whole, facilitates the development of new ideas and solutions, but, in all cases and at all levels, it is imperative that qualified personnel be appointed as its members. Because its efforts and solutions will affect the future of the organization, its members must be inventive, responsible, and willing to initiate and open-mindedly assess new solutions and new ways of problem solving.

Its directness, and the close proximity of its members and components, allows the interdisciplinary planning team to function with optimum efficiency. Repetition of activity and project delays are virtually eliminated. These characteristics combine to diminish the total time period required for the project, thereby reducing the overall project cost. But, again, it should be emphasized that the team's progress ultimately depends on its members.

Planning
for the
Organization

The office landscape concept can be applied to most organizations, regardless of size; however, a medium-sized planning project is not only an ideal example for the purposes of this section but also the most typical application of office landscaping. In the context of this book, a medium-sized project may include all or part of an organization, and comprises approximately 150 to 500 persons. A project within this range may be planned by an interdisciplinary team the size and structure of that described in Section Two. Larger and smaller projects call for team and procedural variations which will be discussed at the end of this section. Again, it is important to remember that the majority of the planning steps explained in this section occur simultaneously, and not sequentially as they are presented.

PLANNING THE PLANNING

Before any detailed planning can be undertaken, it must itself be organized and planned for by accomplishing a few basic and very important steps, which constitute *planning the planning*. Assuming that the organization has selected an outside consultant experienced in the office landscape approach, the first step taken by the consultant should be to familiarize himself/herself with the organization's functions and personnel. This is an obvious procedure if the organization is to be planned for as a whole, and less obvious, though equally necessary, if the planning project incorporates only a part of the organization, because the planning will still affect and indirectly involve the internal and external relationships of the entire organization. In order to minimize confusion arising from possible distinctions between the whole organization and the planned-for group, the latter will be referred to as a *department*.

NOTE: *An outside consultant is normally necessary for the planning of a first installation. If the organization is involved in its second or third installation, chances are good that the experience previously gained by the organization's planning personnel will eliminate the need for an outside office landscape consultant.*

In order to become familiar with and assess the ex-

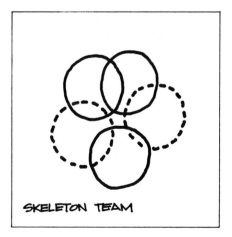

OFFICE LANDSCAPING
IS FOR

SMALL
MEDIUM
LARGE

ORGANIZATIONS

THE
PLANNING
MUST BE
PLANNED

SKELETON TEAM

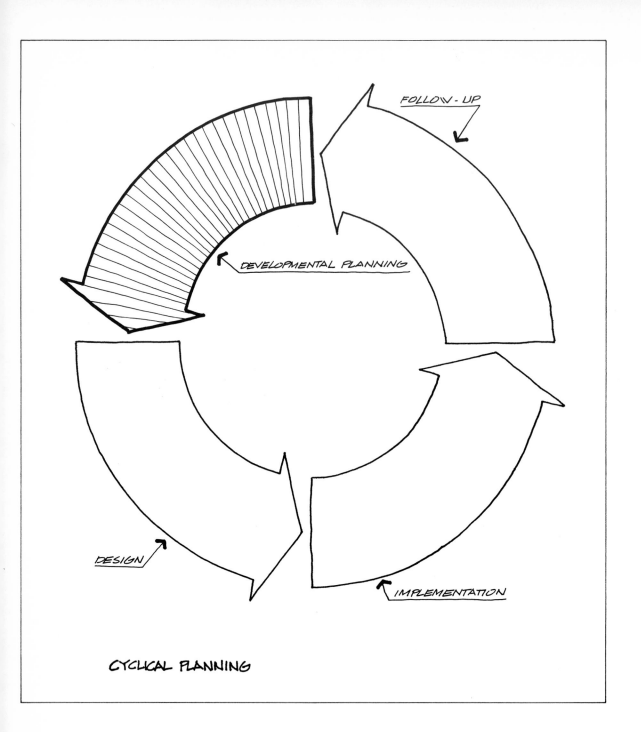

FOLLOW-UP

DEVELOPMENTAL PLANNING

DESIGN

IMPLEMENTATION

CYCLICAL PLANNING

isting department and its function within the organization, the office landscape consultant must have access to its workings and personnel. This is acquired through the knowledge and assistance of members of a temporary *skeleton team.* Besides the outside consultant, this preliminary planning team consists of two people: a member of the planned-for department and a receptionist–clerk-typist, both of whom are chosen by the consultant in agreement with the department's management, and should become members of the larger planning team upon its establishment.

The department member chosen for the skeleton team, who will later become the major liaison between the planning team and the department, should be highly respected within the department and familiar with its operations and personnel, and should have access to all levels of its staff and management. In addition, if possible, this person should eventually coordinate post-follow-up planning within the department and any future office landscape planning which may occur in another subunit of the organization. The selection of this team member, then, is critical; she/he must be inventive and open to new processes and solutions. Often, departmental management seems to feel that only a young person could be suitable, but this is an "ageist" idea and has been disproved time after time.

The receptionist–clerk-typist, unlike the department member, is not necessary to the skeleton team during the office landscape consultant's initial familiarization with the department and organization as a whole. However, after enough information has been gathered to begin establishing goals, strategies, and priorities, and problem detection analysis, his/her full involvement is needed.

Goals, strategies, and priorities, and *problem detection analysis* are two of the first planning steps, and should be outlined by the skeleton team as early as is feasible, in order to provide a general definition of and direction for the planning. This, in turn, allows the team to prepare a preliminary planning *activity time chart.* Although this chart may at first seem formal and unnecessary, it is vital to successful, efficient planning because the project involves the time of every level of department management and staff.

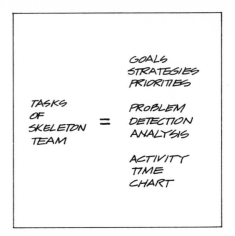

| GOALS | ARE TO SOLVE KNOWN PROBLEMS |

| STRATEGIES | ARE THE MEANS TO THE GOALS |

| STRATEGIES | DEPEND ON GOALS AND PRIORITIES |

It is helpful, though not mandatory, for the discussion and formulation of goals, strategies, and priorities, and problem detection analysis, to take place in the room reserved for planning activities. This establishes the planning room as the center of project activities. The skeleton team should also encourage all personnel to visit the planning room at any time and participate freely in the planning process.

GOALS, STRATEGIES, AND PRIORITIES

Goals, strategies, and priorities are the parameters established for the planning project, and can range from simple statements to detailed sets of ends and means. They should be discussed and mutually determined by the skeleton team and key management of the planned-for department.

NOTE: *It is likely that the goals, strategies, and priorities determined during the early planning stages will need revision after review by the planning team, in light of additional information and input from problem detection analysis, and specialists.*

Goals can encompass any number of different aspects of departmental operation: better environment and public image, easier access to information, more efficient work-flow processes, reduction of overtime and personnel turnover, deregimentation of report and command lines, reorganization of team tasks, inclusion of more sophisticated information-handling equipment, reassessment of status, and so forth. Usually, it is not difficult to determine the goals of the project and define the scope of the planning. For example, in a planning project for a certain department which presently has 200 employees, is growing at the rate of 8 percent per year, and has become fragmented, the goals could be to slow personnel growth to align more closely with overall organization growth, to bring the fragmented department together in an environment of better communication and work flow, and to reduce the quantity of paper/files which is expanding much faster than either the organization or the department.

The office landscape approach is itself a strategy whose foundation is concurrent consideration of and planning for all the department's interrelated elements, both internal and external. The strategies devised to accomplish the project are dependent on the scope and intended depth of the planning, that is, how deeply any or all of the department's four basic elements are to be delved into. This, in turn, is dependent on the time allotted for planning. Many of the planning activities discussed later in this book are strategies: problem detection analysis, communication analysis, correlation diagram, filing system analysis, etc. Strategies are simply the means employed to gather, correlate, and evaluate any information required for planning solutions.

Formulating strategies is vital to the project, but the strategies themselves are dictated by goals and priorities. Though they are presented sequentially here, goals, strategies, and priorities are actually discussed and established concurrently, in open, brainstorming planning sessions. With the aid of a blackboard or chart paper, a group can arrange, rearrange, add, delete, and evaluate department problems and planning factors until a logical, comprehensive set of goals, strategies, and priorities emerges.

PRIORITIES   MUST
               BE
               ESTABLISHED
               EARLY

Priorities generally relate to time. If improved communication is more important to a department than greater filing efficiency, then communication planning takes precedence over filing system planning. Or, for example, if the design of a facility must be completed in time to begin construction on a particular date, planning for the facility must be scheduled as a priority item.

Too often, priorities are overlooked in the early planning stages and surface later, creating planning scheduling problems. The importance of receiving and considering input from all key members of the department cannot be overstated. And the mutual determination of goals and strategies, as well as priorities, by key department personnel and the skeleton team is equally important. Further, the skeleton team's resultant ideas, plans, and conclusions should be presented to all personnel of the planned-for department, that is, the users, for their review and comment. Goals, strategies, and priorities have usually been determined by about two weeks into the project, and by this time, rumors have probably begun to fly throughout the department. This is an opportune time to hold a meeting with the users to present planning ideas, encourage feedback, and ensure the involvement of all users in the project.

Normally, this meeting begins with a general summary of the office landscape approach. Preliminary goals, strategies, and priorities are discussed; upcoming planning steps, such as the chart of hierarchy and function survey (discussed later in this section), are outlined; continuing involvement in planning activities by the users is encouraged; and questions, of course, are answered.

NOTE: *A question that invariably arises during the first meeting with the entire department is whether or not the planning will lead to open-plan offices. However, because it is still too early to formulate physical, environmental solutions, it is unnecessary to compare the virtues and drawbacks of general office plans. It is much more important to assure the users that they will be continuously involved in the planning, and that their input will help determine the direction the planning will take.*

PROBLEM DETECTION ANALYSIS

Problem detection analysis is a matter of gathering information through user interviews and identifying known and previously unknown problems which must be planned for and resolved. The skeleton team must understand the existing organization structure in order to select the users to be interviewed, because, normally, time does not permit interviewing all the individuals in the department. Users must be chosen from every level of the department, and the existing organization chart is usually very helpful in determining the specific people to be involved. The important point here is to select a cross section of the department, or the results of problem detection analysis will be lopsided and will not reflect all the problems that need solutions. In a department of 200 people, approximately one-third should be interviewed, and the interviewees should be chosen and informed of their selection far enough in advance to allow them to discuss possible departmental problems with their colleagues prior to

PROBLEM DETECTION ANALYSIS / SAMPLE LAYOUT

CATEGORY/SUBCATEGORY	FACT	HYPOTHESIS	WISH
1/ORGANIZATION			
PROGRAM	☐☐☐ ☐	☐	☐☐☐☐ ☐☐
PROCEDURES	☐	☐☐☐☐	
COORDINATION	☐	☐☐	☐☐☐☐ ☐
	☐☐		
2/PERSONNEL			
HIRING	☐☐	☐	☐☐
TRAINING	☐	☐☐☐	
SCREENING	☐	☐ ☐☐	☐☐
COMPENSATION	☐☐ ☐		☐
PROMOTION	☐ ☐	☐	☐☐☐☐ ☐☐☐☐
3/INFORMATION			
GENERAL	☐☐	☐	
MEMORANDUMS	☐ ☐☐	☐☐	☐☐
MAIL AND FILES	☐ ☐	☐☐ ☐☐	☐ ☐ ☐☐
4/ENVIRONMENT/EQUIPMENT			
PERSONAL WORKPLACE	☐ ☐	☐	☐☐☐☐
ORGANIZATION IMAGE	☐	☐	☐☐☐☐

FACTS ARE STATEMENTS WHICH CAN BE VERIFIED

HYPOTHESES ARE HARD TO PROVE STATEMENTS

WISHES ARE SOMETIMES EXPRESSED AS QUESTIONS

the interviews. Should the information gathered tend to be redundant, the number of interviews can be reduced, or if the information tends to be unrelated, the number can be increased. However, in either case, a balance of supervisors and staff should be maintained.

Essentially, problem detection analysis is an interview between planner and user to identify the department's negative aspects, or problems. The principal purpose of the office landscape approach, and, one assumes, the planning project, is finding and solving problems. Positive aspects of the department do not need as much attention as negative ones, and if positive as well as negative data are sought, the task of correlating information is compounded.

During their interviews, department personnel talk about their jobs, relationships with coworkers, the problems they see within the organization, and how these problems might be rectified. As the discussion proceeds, the team member records pertinent information, subsequently to be arranged in categories of *facts, hypotheses,* and *wishes.*

Facts are statements which can be verified. For example, a person might say that she/he could get more accomplished each day if the files needed for a certain task were together and not in three locations, or that because her/his office is at the department entrance, she/he is constantly interrupted by persons outside the department asking for directions. These examples are facts and can be proved by simple observation.

Hypotheses are statements which may be factual, but which either cannot be proved or cannot be proved easily, such as the statement that middle- and lower-level staff are not informed of overall departmental operations, or that departments tend to duplicate tasks.

Wishes are basically the desires that an employee has, and are sometimes expressed as questions. For instance, the user might say that he/she would like to know for sure who his/her supervisor is or that salaries and raises should be made public within the department and based on objective criteria, or ask why he/she is not a member of the auditing group although he/she works with it most of the time.

NOTE: *First-time planners will probably want to sit in*

PROBLEM DETECTION ANALYSIS / SAMPLE SUMMARY

CATEGORY/SUBCATEGORY	FACT	HYPOTHESIS	WISH
2/PERSONNEL			
SCREENING	THERE IS NO FORMAL SCREENING OF PERSONNEL		
HIRING		SOME EMPLOYEES BELIEVE THEY SHOULD BE GIVEN CONTRACTS	CONTRACTS SHOULD GUARANTEE EMPLOYMENT FOR ONE YEAR
TRAINING	THE ONLY TRAINING IS ON-THE-JOB TRAINING	FORMAL TRAINING PROGRAM SHOULD BE ESTABLISHED	STAFF DEVELOPMENT PROGRAM SHOULD BE CONSIDERED
COMPENSATION	SALARY STRUCTURE IS NOT CONSISTENT AMONG DEPARTMENTS	RAISES SHOULD BE ANNOUNCED AND BASED ON OBJECTIVE CRITERIA	
	SALARY STRUCTURE IS NOT CONSISTENT AMONG INDIVIDUALS. WOMEN ARE DISCRIMINATED AGAINST		FRINGE BENEFITS SHOULD BE MORE CONSISTENT
PROMOTIONS	THERE ARE NO CRITERIA OR PROCEDURES FOR PROMOTIONS		
REWARDS	THERE IS NO MERIT RATING SYSTEM		NONMONETARY REWARDS WOULD BE A GOOD WAY TO EXPRESS RECOGNITION
TERMINATION		SOME EMPLOYEES SUSPECT THAT THERE IS A NONFIRING POLICY. UNWANTED PERSONNEL ARE DISCRIMINATED AGAINST UNTIL THEY CHOOSE TO LEAVE	
PROCEDURES	THERE IS NO FRAMEWORK OR POLICY FOR SELECTING, TRAINING, EVALUATING, OR REWARDING EMPLOYEES		PERFORMANCE EVALUATION SHOULD BE BASIS FOR MANAGING PERSONNEL
		SOME EMPLOYEES SUSPECT THAT THERE IS A TENDENCY TO AVOID SETTING STANDARDS	
QUALIFICATIONS	SOME EMPLOYEES ARE ASSIGNED DUTIES OUTSIDE THEIR QUALIFICATIONS	AVAILABLE MANPOWER COULD BE USED MORE EFFICIENTLY	PERFORMANCE AND PERSONAL CAPABILITIES SHOULD BE EVALUATED PERIODICALLY

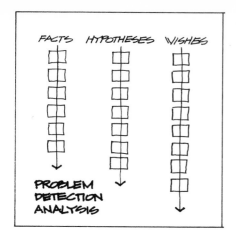

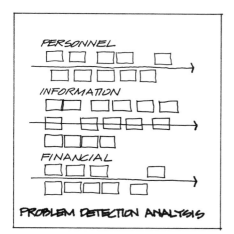

on interviews conducted by the outside planning consultant until they get the gist of interview techniques and can proceed to conduct separate interviews on their own.

It is not necessary for each fact to have an accompanying or related hypothesis and wish; or each hypothesis, a fact and wish, etc. Each item may stand on its own, and the likelihood is that data from one person will correlate with data from others.

After the information is gathered in the problem detection interviews, it must be arranged in a usable form. There are probably a number of ways to organize the material, but an easy straightforward process is a matrix of vertical and horizontal categories. If the information received in interview sessions was not recorded on index cards, it should be transferred to them, one statement to a card, with an appropriate notation of fact, hypothesis, or wish, the three vertical categories.

To separate the cards into horizontal categories, it is necessary to be somewhat familiar with the information. Cards with statements on similar subjects should be grouped together. Groups may be classified and subclassified. Major categories might be organization, personnel, information, office environment and equipment, external environment, financial aspects, etc.; and subcategories of personnel, for example, might be hiring, training, screening, compensation, promotion, reward, termination of employment, procedures, qualifications, minority groups, job descriptions, turnover, attitudes, etc. The more categories and subcategories, the easier the information will be to assess.

With both the vertical and horizontal categories defined, the insertion of information into the matrix becomes a simple task. If the cards are pinned to a wall or spread on a table, the data can be arranged and rearranged until the matrix has taken final form. And when the matrix is complete, departmental problems will be readily apparent. Probably, a number of cards will carry essentially the same information, immediately emphasizing a particular area of concern. And just as groups of cards with similar data should not be overlooked, neither should a card which does not fit in a group be disregarded, because it is not uncommon for an astute person to pinpoint a major problem overlooked by others.

Obviously, several hundred cards, whether on a table or a wall, will be difficult to manage, and so a summary of the information gathered is recommended. Usually, a summary maintains the major categories of organization, personnel, etc., and describes pertinent groups of facts, hypotheses, and wishes with single statements. It is imperative that members of the planned-for department and other key members of the organization review the matrix before summaries are concluded to ensure their understanding of and participation in the planning process.

The information gathered in problem detection analysis is valuable because it comes from all levels of the department, identifying and emphasizing problems which could easily be overlooked by planners, especially outside consultants and key management. Not only does problem detection analysis point out areas for planning activities, but it often expands or alters goals, strategies, and priorities.

ACTIVITY TIME CHART

The activity time chart is similar to a CPM or PERT network plan, though usually not as sophisticated. Its purpose is to indicate all planning activities, their starting and completion dates, interdependencies, and the persons or groups responsible for their accomplishment. The priorities established earlier by the skeleton team should be followed in drawing up the chart, but it is possible that they will need to be altered as activities and time frames are established and detailed.

The chart primarily represents the planning activities of the office landscape planning team; however, it must also include activities which are the responsibility of persons outside the actual planning team. For example, if competitive bids are to be taken for new furniture and equipment, furniture manufacturers must be given adequate lead time to prepare and submit bids, and to produce, deliver, and install their products; or, if a move-in date is absolutely fixed, the telephone company must have advance notification of its responsibilities. In either of these examples, a com-

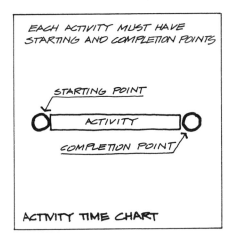

PROBLEM DETECTION ANALYSIS
MAY EXPAND
GOALS STRATEGIES PRIORITIES

THE ACTIVITY TIME CHART IS A SCHEDULE OF CONCURRENT INTERDEPENDENT PLANNING ACTIVITIES

EACH ACTIVITY MUST HAVE STARTING AND COMPLETION POINTS

STARTING POINT
ACTIVITY
COMPLETION POINT

ACTIVITY TIME CHART

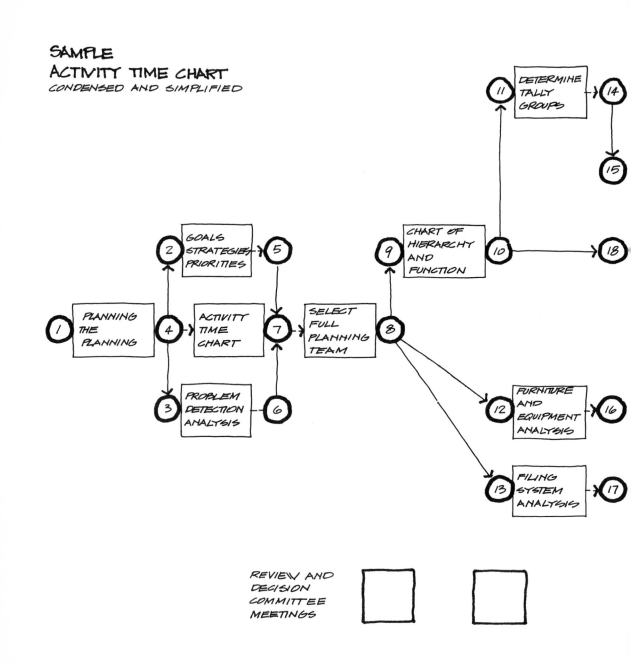

SAMPLE
ACTIVITY TIME CHART
CONDENSED AND SIMPLIFIED

REVIEW AND
DECISION
COMMITTEE
MEETINGS

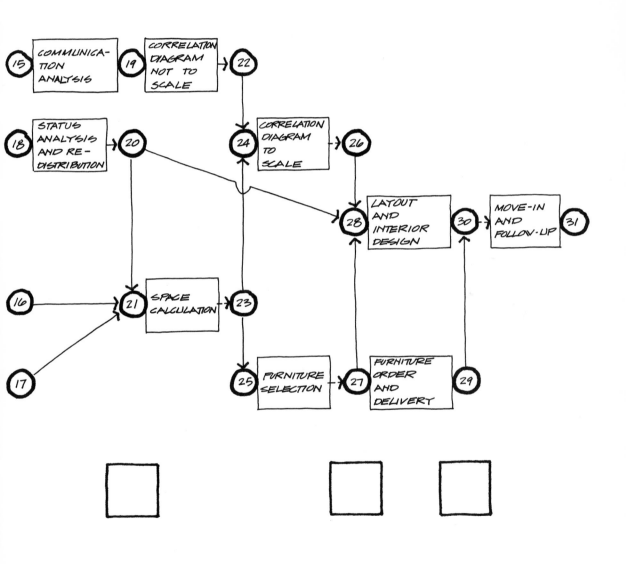

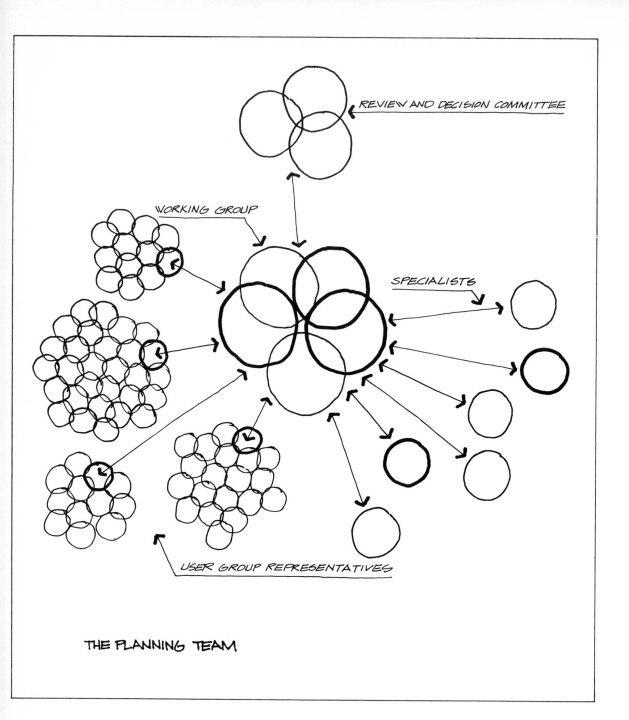

REVIEW AND DECISION COMMITTEE

WORKING GROUP

SPECIALISTS

USER GROUP REPRESENTATIVES

THE PLANNING TEAM

pany representative should be involved in the project early enough to have input into the planning, as well as to prepare for the installation.

Each activity and activity subdivision must have its own chart line, and a starting and completion point. Though it is not always done, numbering starting and completion points provides a sequential system which can be checked off to eliminate oversight.

An activity requiring two weeks' working time may begin in the third week of planning, so that certain information from that activity can be used in the fourth or fifth week; however, the total activity may not need to be completed until the fourteenth week. This non-active period is called *float time,* and is usually shown on the chart as a dotted line or a line of lesser weight than that of the actual working time needed for the task.

For clarity, activity time charts are often laid out in colors, each color representing a different discipline or area of responsibility. And, although rare, the activities of certain complex disciplines can be shown alongside the office landscape planning activities. For instance, charts of architectural and planning activities might be presented adjacent to each other.

The activity time chart is a planning tool and therefore must not be absolutely rigid. The chart, like the planning itself, must be flexible enough to permit alterations and allow expansion and contraction of activities. However, the overall completion date can remain unaltered if the midportion of the schedule provides adequate float time.

In addition to graphically representing various planning activities, the chart also graphically indicates the disciplines necessary to accomplish these activities. Consequently, the chart is a valuable aid in designing the total planning team.

PLANNING TEAM

Given completion of goals, strategies, and priorities, problem detection analysis, and the activity time chart, enough information has been gathered to establish most of the planning team. The working group, specialists, and review and decision committee can be selected, though the user group representatives should

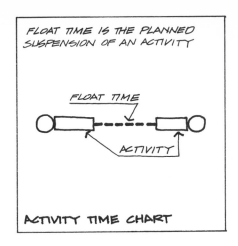

FLOAT TIME IS THE PLANNED SUSPENSION OF AN ACTIVITY

FLOAT TIME

ACTIVITY

ACTIVITY TIME CHART

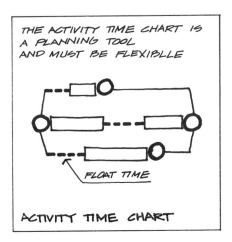

THE ACTIVITY TIME CHART IS A PLANNING TOOL AND MUST BE FLEXIBLLE

FLOAT TIME

ACTIVITY TIME CHART

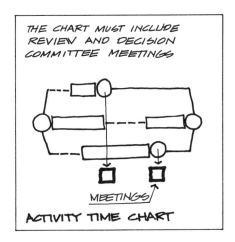

THE CHART MUST INCLUDE REVIEW AND DECISION COMMITTEE MEETINGS

MEETINGS

ACTIVITY TIME CHART

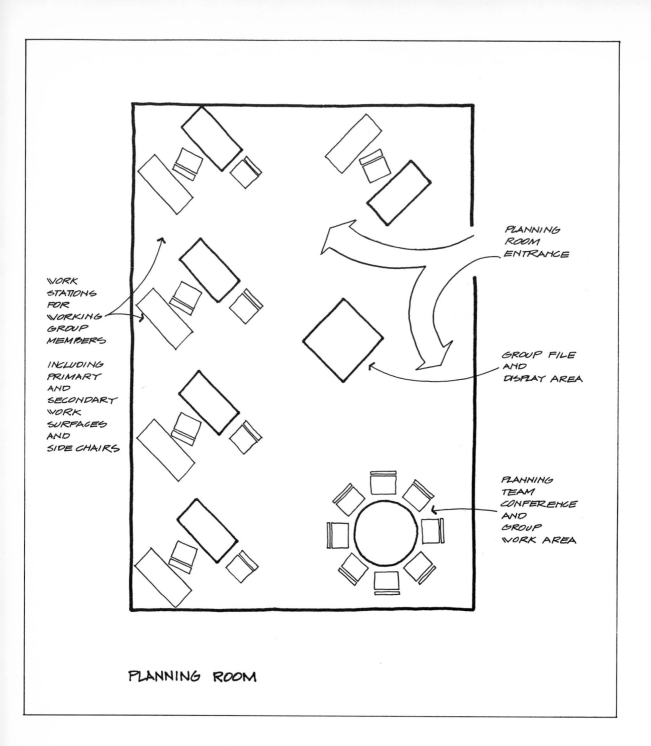

WORK
STATIONS
FOR
WORKING
GROUP
MEMBERS

INCLUDING
PRIMARY
AND
SECONDARY
WORK
SURFACES
AND
SIDE CHAIRS

PLANNING
ROOM
ENTRANCE

GROUP FILE
AND
DISPLAY AREA

PLANNING
TEAM
CONFERENCE
AND
GROUP
WORK AREA

PLANNING ROOM

be chosen after additional information has been received from the chart of hierarchy and function survey.

In Section Two, "Complexity of Planning," the planning team is discussed in some detail, and so only a summary is provided here. The working group consists of about five people, including the outside office landscape consultant. This group is responsible for organizing and accomplishing the overall planning project.

The specialists include in-house and outside consultants, each of whom is expert in a particular discipline necessary to the success of the project and is responsible to the working group for the planning activities related to her/his discipline.

The review and decision committee is composed of high-level department and organization personnel. Its function is to review and become familiar with planning activities and progress, and to render and/or endorse decisions as needed.

The user group consists of representatives of departmental subelements, each representative serving as a liaison between team and department.

One of the first tasks of the planning team, either in full session or preferably in small groups, is to review previous planning activities, especially the activity time chart, since it not only reflects goals, strategies, and priorities, and the results of problem detection analysis, but also specifies the responsibilities of all the team members, activity interdependencies, and time allotments.

An ideal way to handle this initial planning review is for the working group to meet with the specialists and user group separately, alter the activity time chart as required, and present the revised chart to the review and decision committee.

NOTE: *An inherent problem in working with any group or individual responsible for decision making is a lack of preparation on the decision maker's part. In order to ensure valuable, informed decisions, the working group should insist that the members of the review and decision committee visit the planning room as often as possible to observe the planning process, and that committee meetings include agendas of future meetings.*

THE PLANNING TEAM SHOULD REVIEW PLANNING THE PLANNING

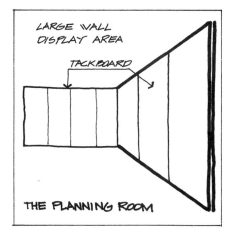

THE PLANNING ROOM GIVES USERS "ANYTIME" ACCESS TO THE PLANNING

LARGE WALL DISPLAY AREA

TACKBOARD

THE PLANNING ROOM

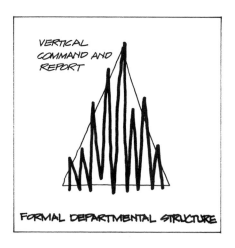

VERTICAL COMMAND AND REPORT

FORMAL DEPARTMENTAL STRUCTURE

PLANNING ROOM

Certainly one of the most important tools in the office landscape planning process is the *planning room*. As the center of planning activities, it provides the users with easy access to the planning team and its progress.

In addition to individual workplaces for the full-time working group members, the planning room should have a conference area for group meetings and discussions, filing and storage space for planning materials, and, above all, a large wall display area for diagrams, matrices, charts, etc. It is also advantageous to have additional workplaces for one or two specialists, a drafting area for layouts and models, and an expandable conference area for large meetings, though these are not mandatory.

Since the planning room is a work tool, flexibility should be stressed. Each planning project will require its team to function a little differently, and the setup needed will vary. Depending on the project, one planning room may function well with only the minimum requirements, and another may need slide and overhead projectors, chalkboards, chart boards, dictation equipment, and perhaps an auxiliary room for display of furniture and furnishings being considered for use in the planned-for space. In either case, because the tasks of the working group and the specialists are interdependent and take place concurrently, team members need immediate access to each other and the information they require.

CHART OF HIERARCHY AND FUNCTION

Within most departments, there is a formal and an informal structure. The formal structure of the department is usually described by an organization chart or plan, which represents persons and/or functions in stacked boxes, connected to vertical lines representing, top to bottom, the power to command or the right to issue directives and, bottom to top, the obligation to report. The formal structure narrows the individual's behavioral possibilities and conducts her/him along predetermined routes. It clearly defines positions, tasks, power, and status by the standardization of behavior.

However, the organization chart almost never reflects or coincides with what actually happens within the department. The informal structure, on the other hand, corrects the unrealistic rigidity of the formal by considering the functional requirements of the individual, his/her abilities, interests, likes, dislikes, needs, and goals. Consequently, the formal organization is in conflict with the informal. For example, in any department there are instances of people listed in, say, the fourth level of the organization chart who have direct anytime access to the department head. This is contrary to the formal plan. There are even more examples of persons listed in a certain position/group on the organization chart who spend most of their time in a slot shown half a chart away, or even with people in another department.

It is therefore necessary to establish a *chart of hierarchy and function* which illustrates the informal structure, its lines of communication, and the real grouping of departmental personnel. This information could be gathered in interviews, but these are time-consuming. Therefore a combination of questionnaires and spot interviews is recommended.

The questionnaire's design is important, and while its immediate purpose is to gain information related to work assignments and contacts, additional information should also be gathered at this time to minimize later interference with personnel work time. The questionnaire should seek the following: personnel information, such as name, room, telephone, job title, branch unit, and immediate supervisor; job information, which includes the estimated percentages of time the employee spends at and away from her/his desk, and at the various types of work she/he is involved in; paper work, which relates to the types of paper work the person is most involved with; and contacts, which simply show the employee's most frequent contacts with others. Clearly, most of the data collected under job information and paper work are not related to the chart of hierarchy and function, but will be necessary to design workplace types and filing systems.

All members of the planned-for department must complete the questionnaire. During the meeting of the skeleton team and the users, described earlier, this questionnaire should be discussed and its importance

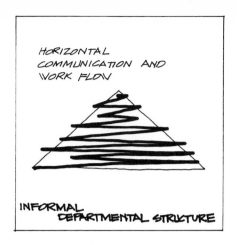

HORIZONTAL COMMUNICATION AND WORK FLOW

INFORMAL DEPARTMENTAL STRUCTURE

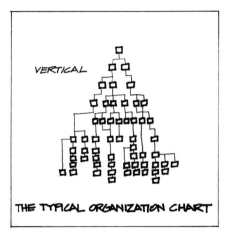

VERTICAL

THE TYPICAL ORGANIZATION CHART

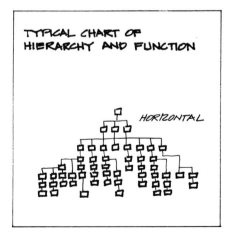

TYPICAL CHART OF HIERARCHY AND FUNCTION

HORIZONTAL

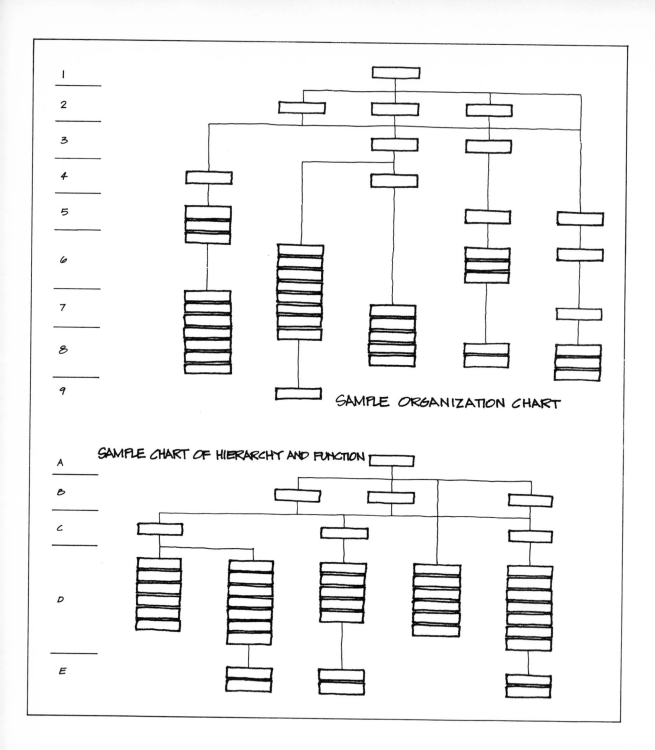

SAMPLE ORGANIZATION CHART

SAMPLE CHART OF HIERARCHY AND FUNCTION

emphasized to ensure personnel cooperation. Correct data are imperative, and spot checks for authenticity should be conducted by members of the working team while the employees have the questionnaire.

The chart of hierarchy and function is determined from questionnaire information, and invariably deviates from the organization chart. The most notable deviation is in the number of departmental levels. It is not uncommon for the informal chart to have half as many levels as the organization chart.

After the chart of hierarchy and function has been developed, it must be tested for accuracy. Since this chart and the organization chart are both graphic representations, they can be compared side by side, or by transparent overlay. Further, the new chart must be reviewed and discussed with the user group and the review and decision committee, and appropriate alterations made.

NOTE: *In many instances, where planning involves a total organization, the chart of hierarchy and function will replace the existing organization chart. However, where the planned-for department is a piece of an organization which consists of several departments, and in which personnel levels, pay scales, etc., are related throughout the organization, discarding the existing chart is dangerous unless a separate planning activity, involving all departments, is undertaken to establish a comprehensive chart of hierarchy and function.*

On the basis of the chart of hierarchy and function, the planning team can establish subunits within the department. The number of subunits that emerges depends, of course, on the given department and planning project. A department with sixteen subunits is represented in the illustration "Sample Chart of Hierarchy and Function."

The subunits serve several purposes: they subdivide the department into logical units of manageable size for the working group and its planning activities; they form the framework for selecting user group representatives to the planning team; and they establish *tally groups* which include and identify each departmental employee.

A tally group is identical to a subunit or subgroup. Each tally group carefully selects a representative who

TALLY
GROUPS
SELECT
USER
GROUP
REPRESENTATIVES
FOR
THE
PLANNING
TEAM

DETERMINE TALLY GROUPS
FROM CHART OF HIERARCHY AND FUNCTION

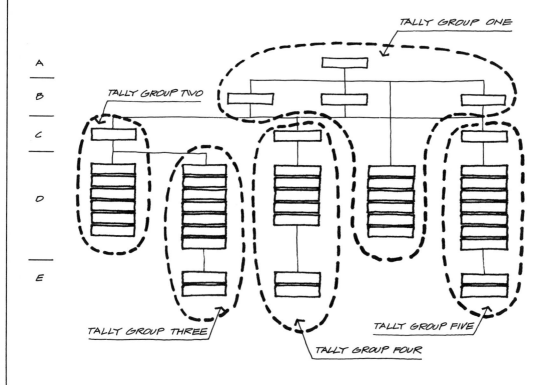

WORK/TIME DISTRIBUTION
PERCENTAGES FROM INDIVIDUAL ESTIMATES

JOB TITLE	A	B	C	D	E
NUMBER OF PERSONS	1	3	30	60	20
PERCENTAGE OF WORK/TIME AT DESK	40	60	50	50	30
PERCENTAGE OF WORK/TIME AT TYPEWRITER	–	–	–	35	45
PERCENTAGE OF WORK/TIME AT OTHER MACHINES	–	–	10	–	5
PERCENTAGE OF TIME MEETING AT DESK	20	20	20	5	5
PERCENTAGE OF TIME AWAY FROM DESK	40	20	20	10	15

becomes a member of the planning team user group. This person should be able to understand and articulate the needs of each member of his/her tally group.

NOTE: *Invariably, the highest ranking person in a group is considered for the representative position. If this person is in a supervisory slot and tends to speak only for management, others should be considered. In some planned-for departments, rules are established that no supervisory personnel can be representatives. Although the intent of these rules is understandable, they can backfire, causing user groups to represent only staff. In any case, each representative should be carefully selected to speak for every member of her/his group.*

After the tally groups have been established and their representatives selected, each member of the department can be given an identifying number or symbol. Usually numbers are easier to work with, especially as the planning progresses and the working group must handle communication analysis and related information. The intention of using numbers is certainly not to depersonalize individuals, but merely to simplify recording information received from the members of the department.

NOTE: *If there are sixteen tally groups, each may be assigned a round number such as 100, 200, . . ., 1,600, and each tally group member a 1, 2, or 3, and so on. This allows 812 or 1,106 to identify not only the employee, but also the employee's tally group.*

A *work/time distribution matrix* can also be derived from the information on the questionnaires. This matrix records the types of functions performed at workplaces and estimates the amounts of time spent on each function.

This information, to be supported later in the planning by further investigations, will serve as a basis for determining the proper furniture, furnishings, and equipment for each workplace.

The matrix is a combination of the job title/job function levels established by the chart of hierarchy and function, and the work/time distribution percentages documented on the survey questionnaires. The matrix indicates job titles, number of persons listed under specific job titles, and percentages of time spent on various work tasks. Wherever job title categories

SAMPLE
TALLY SHEET

NAME _____

TALLY GROUP NUMBER _____

INSIDE CONTACTS

PERSONS IN TALLY GROUP	TALLY GROUP NO.	NUMBER OF TELEPHONE CALLS RECEIVED	TOTAL	NUMBER OF PAPERS RECEIVED	TOTAL	NUMBER OF VISITS AND/OR CONFERENCES	TOTAL
J. BISHOP W. WALDROP D. OLSON P. LEAF L. BROTHERTON J. BROWN	01						
B. FERGUSON J. HILDRETH C. SNYPP D. BOWEN R. TOMAI R. PASTON C. WRIGHT J. CANINE J. SELDOMRIDGE	02						
D. LENCE J. COLEMAN J. MUSACHIO B. SHORT	03						
L. BENNETT D. MESSERSMITH J. BRONSON O. OLSON JR. BROWN D. LEAF	04						

OUTSIDE CONTACTS

CONTACT GROUP	CODE	CONTACTS RECEIVED			CONTACTS MADE		
		TELEPHONE	PAPER	VISITS CONF.	TELEPHONE	PAPER	VISITS CONF.
EASTERN REGION OFFICE	NY						
WESTERN REGION OFFICE	SF						
OTHER							
OTHER							

involve several persons whose percentages of work/time distribution are not compatible, then either an individual has made a mistake on the questionnaire and must be interviewed, or the information is correct and a new job title category must be established. For instance, a mail clerk might have the same job title as certain other people within the department, but might, by virtue of different tasks and work/time distribution, require a new job title category.

COMMUNICATION ANALYSIS

Communication analysis is without a doubt one of the most important planning phases. In order to achieve a high efficiency level in office work, individual workplaces and tally groups must be arranged according to the intensity of their interactions. Communication analysis measures these interactions.

Although communication along hierarchical or vertical lines is extremely important, it differs drastically from horizontal communication in terms of frequency. Both the vertical and horizontal must be considered in space arrangements, and therefore it is essential to analyze and understand the department's communication patterns thoroughly.

Communication analysis consists of a *communication tally* which translates into a *matrix of interactions*.

NOTE: *Some office planner-designers feel that a communication tally is unnecessary and that the user survey questionnaire provides adequate data for designing ideal workplace arrangements. However, experience indicates not only that employees are often surprised by the results of communication tallies— therefore invalidating questionnaire information to some extent—but also that, without the matrix of interactions, it is not possible to quantify and qualify the department's communication.*

Essentially, a communication tally is a detailed measurement of a group's communication during a given period of time. The tally involves every member of the department and includes three types of communication: telephone interaction, paper interaction, and personal visit interaction. The tally simply involves logging incoming and outgoing communications in the three categories.

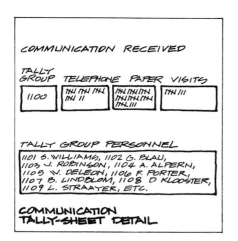

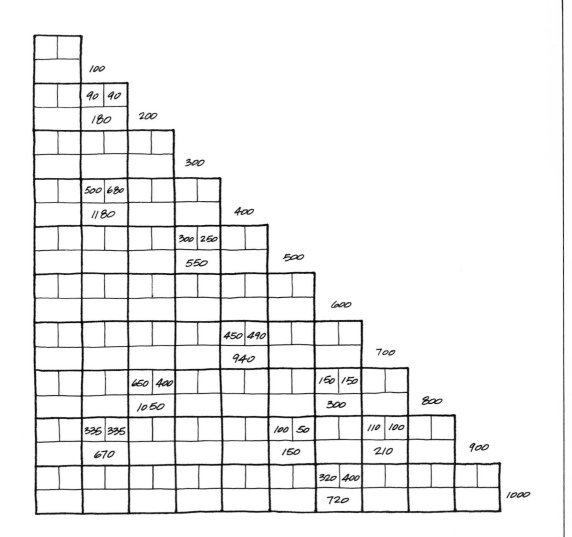

SAMPLE MATRIX OF TOTAL COMMUNICATIONS

TOTAL TELEPHONE, PAPER, AND VISITS COMBINED

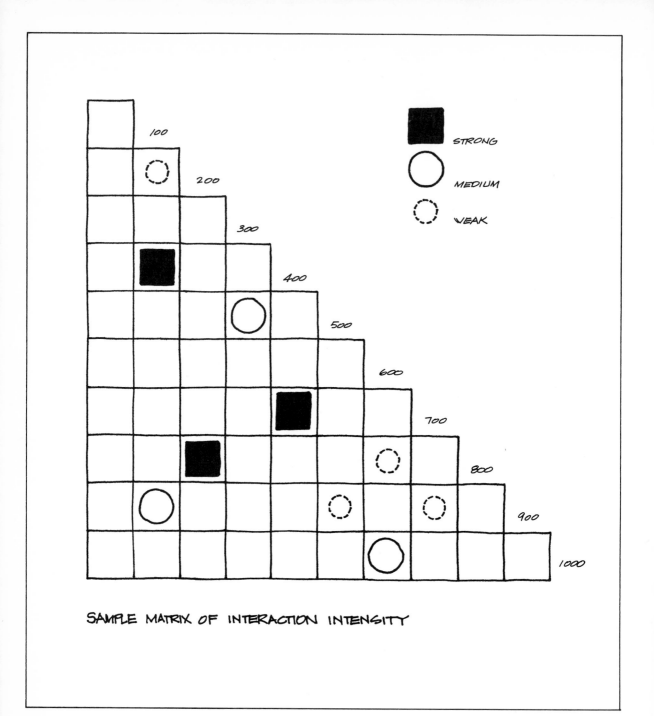

SAMPLE MATRIX OF INTERACTION INTENSITY

Obviously, all received and transmitted communication could be recorded; however, this increases the time involvement of both the department employees in recording communications, and the working group in sorting out the data. Recording only transmitted communications does not work simply because data coming into the department from outside are missed. Consequently, the easiest method for all concerned is to record communications received from within the department and all communications going out of the department and coming in from outside.

The communication tally is recorded on *tally sheets* given to each member of the department. The user does not record communications from her/his own tally group, but records communications from members of other tally groups under the general heading of that person's group. As each communication is received, or each outside-department communication is transmitted, a mark is placed beside the appropriate tally group and beneath the appropriate type of interaction: telephone, paper, or visit.

The communication tally should be conducted during a representative period of two work weeks, although it should be reviewed in light of vacations and cyclic work tasks within the department.

Any communication by paper is recorded as one interaction whether a single piece of paper or a twenty-page report is received or transmitted. And, it goes without saying, visits not related to departmental business should not be recorded.

With the completion of the communication tally, interactions can be totaled for each tally group. The totals should include an overall total of interactions and three separate totals for interactions by telephone, paper, and visit. This provides four totals for every tally group a given group communicated with.

These totals can be transferred to a matrix of interactions which permits easier assessment of the information. A separate matrix may be developed for each type of interaction: telephone, paper, and visit; or a single matrix of all interactions can be compiled.

The matrix is constructed much like a mileage chart, presenting the interactions between any two tally groups in a square at the intersection of their respective numbers. Each square must contain three

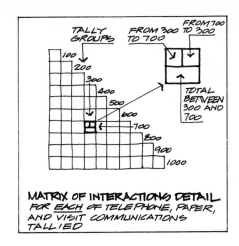

MATRIX OF INTERACTIONS DETAIL
FOR EACH OF TELEPHONE, PAPER, AND VISIT COMMUNICATIONS TALLIED

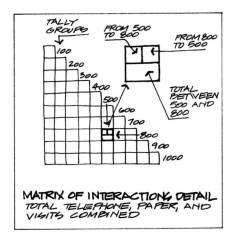

MATRIX OF INTERACTIONS DETAIL
TOTAL TELEPHONE, PAPER, AND VISITS COMBINED

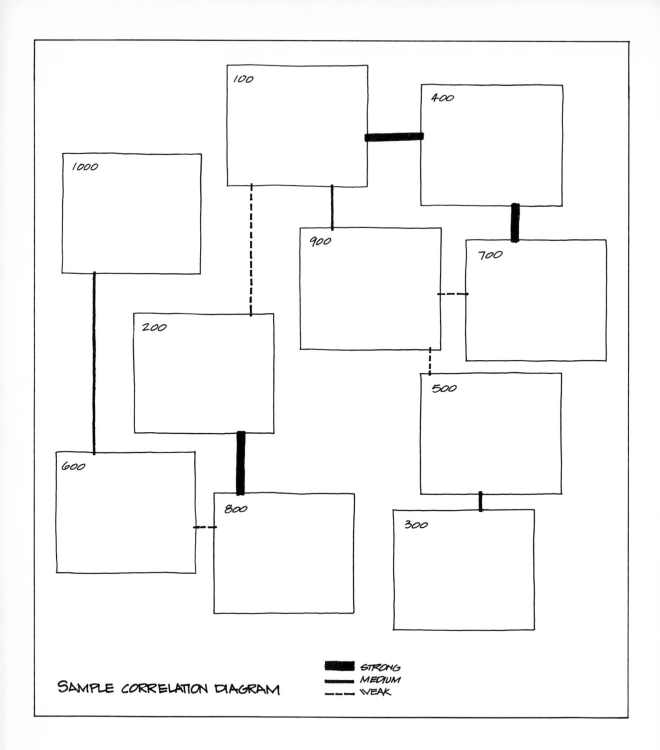

SAMPLE CORRELATION DIAGRAM

STRONG
MEDIUM
---- WEAK

numbers: the totals of interactions from one group to the other and vice versa, and the total of these two figures.

The information contained in the matrix of interactions can be simplified to represent the totals of communication interactions between tally groups. Assume that the least number is 0, and the greatest is 1,200. The intensity of contacts can be categorized as weak, medium, and strong. Weak could be from 0 to 400, medium from 401 to 800, and strong from 801 to 1,200. If separate symbols are assigned to weak, medium, and strong, a *matrix of interaction intensity* can be established showing the communication information in graphic form. Such a matrix is much easier for the planning team to understand, review, and use.

As the planning team assesses the matrix of interaction intensity, it may become apparent that, in a few cases, the importance of communication quantity is altered by the quality of communication. In other words, one tally group may receive very few, but critical, communications which should be given more weight than their numbers would suggest. Because the importance of each communication is not included in the matrix, the planning team must depend on its overall working knowledge of the department in determining which communications are critical and which are not. However, it should be emphasized that deviation from the matrix is justified only in extreme situations.

CORRELATION DIAGRAM IS THE FIRST STEP TOWARD A LOGICAL LAYOUT OF THE DEPARTMENT

CORRELATION DIAGRAM

The *correlation diagram* is a graphic representation of the department by tally groups, indicating the best general spatial relationships of each group to all the others. It is derived from the matrix of interaction intensity and reflects weak, medium, and strong communication patterns. However, it should be pointed out that the correlation diagram is not to scale; that is, all tally groups are shown as the same size.

Each tally group is represented by a rectangle containing the group's number and title. Communication interactions between groups and outside the department are represented by weak, medium, and strong lines, or no lines where there is no communication.

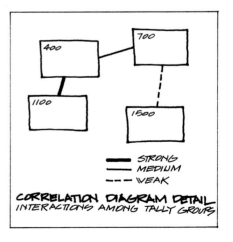

CORRELATION DIAGRAM DETAIL
INTERACTIONS AMONG TALLY GROUPS

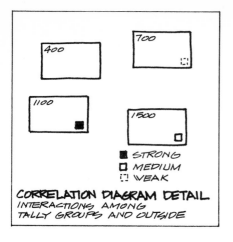

CORRELATION DIAGRAM DETAIL
INTERACTIONS AMONG
TALLY GROUPS AND OUTSIDE

PAPER-FLOW
STUDY
MAY BE
INDICATED
BY
PROBLEM
DETECTION
AND
COMMUNICATION
ANALYSES

FOR
PAPER-
FLOW
STUDY
A
LARGE
COMPLEX
NETWORK
SHOULD
BE
CHOSEN

Colors, rather than different thicknesses and types of lines, are also suitable.

The task of laying out the correlation diagram may appear simple, but it is not because the diagram must show not only the strength of interactions but also the arrangement of tally groups which optimizes these interactions. This means the lines, especially the strong ones, must be as short as possible; that is, the groups with heavy communication interaction must be close together. All interactions must be facilitated. Although it is virtually impossible to design a diagram without one line of communication crossing another, this should be kept to a minimum for reasons which become very clear later in the planning, when additional information is introduced and the diagram layout is to scale.

The correlation diagram is the first step toward a logical spatial layout of the department, and, like all planning activities, it must be presented to, reviewed by, and, if necessary, altered by members of the planning team and the organization.

PAPER-FLOW STUDY

A *paper-flow study* does not have to be a part of the office landscape process; in fact, there are more office landscape projects planned without paper-flow studies than with them. Normally, there are two indications that such a study should be undertaken. First, problem detection analysis may reveal certain information processing problems and duplication of efforts within the department, and second, communication analysis may indicate an unusually high volume of paper flow relative to other types of communication. Communication analysis usually amplifies the trends discovered in problem detection analysis, and the team, after review and discussion, may disregard a high volume of paper communication if no problem is revealed in detection analysis.

If a paper-flow study is indicated, a detailed examination of a typical departmental paper-flow network is warranted. The network selected should be a frequently recurring routine activity, with large volume and complex flow involving as many departmental groups as possible. A paper-flow network satisfying

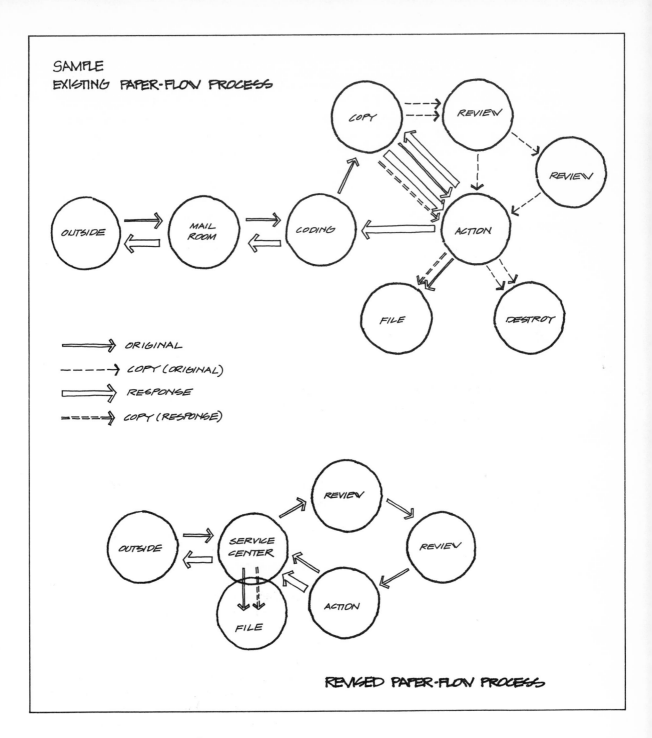

SAMPLE
EXISTING PAPER-FLOW PROCESS

ORIGINAL
COPY (ORIGINAL)
RESPONSE
COPY (RESPONSE)

REVISED PAPER-FLOW PROCESS

PAPER-FLOW STUDY DISPLAY

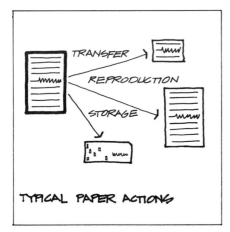

TYPICAL PAPER ACTIONS

these requirements can be pinpointed by examining the paper interactions shown in the communication analysis and by interviewing the key personnel whose groups are involved.

Conducting a paper-flow study is relatively simple though time-consuming. The method is to determine where the selected paper-flow network originates in or enters into the department, and to follow every processing step until the paper leaves the department, or the process is terminated. Each step should be examined in detail, and the papers involved documented, reproduced, and displayed in linear fashion in the planning room.

It is important to document even the smallest processes in the paper-flow network, such as reading and initialing; stamping; transferring certain information to separate forms, tapes, or computer data processing systems; storing; etc. Documentation should also include any actions created by spin-off documents.

There is an interesting phenomenon related to this study. It is that almost any person involved in the network's chain of actions, when questioned only about his/her particular function in the process, can readily and easily explain its purpose. However, when the entire network is graphically displayed, the same person tends to question the value of his/her actions. This is usually because duplication of effort becomes clear when the paper-flow network is viewed as a whole.

With the information available in graphic form, it is relatively easy to analyze and redesign paper flow to achieve a more logical and streamlined process.

NOTE: *In one planning project, a particular paper-flow study revealed that one incoming document required seventy-three separate actions. After review, the process was reduced to three actions without altering the desired results in any way.*

Some duplication of effort is generally created through the initiative of employees trying to do a better job. Initiative must not be quashed, but the creation of new work steps, for whatever reasons, should be viewed from a broader perspective than the individual or group. Possibly an incentive should be introduced to reduce rather than create work steps.

The consequences of a paper-flow study and the resultant streamlined paper-flow network are far-

EXISTING FURNITURE AND EQUIPMENT INVENTORY SUMMARY

ITEM	LEVEL A	LEVEL B	LEVEL C	LEVEL D	LEVEL E	TOTAL
REFRIGERATOR						
TELEVISION						
RADIO						
FLAG						
PLANT AND PLANTER						
DESK / EXECUTIVE, SPECIAL						
DESK / EXECUTIVE 36 X 72						
DESK / EXECUTIVE 36 X 60						
DESK / STANDARD 30 X 60						
DESK / WITH RUNOFF						
DESK / 30 X 45						
CREDENZA / 20 X 60						
CREDENZA / 24 X 72						
MACHINE TABLE / 20 X 20						
MACHINE TABLE / 20 X 30						
CHAIR / LARGE DESK						
CHAIR / SMALL DESK						
CHAIR / CONFERENCE						
CHAIR / STENO						
CHAIR / SIDE, UPHOLSTERED						
CHAIR / SIDE, WOODEN						
CHAIR / SIDE, FOLDING						
FILE / 2 DRAWER LETTER						
FILE / 2 DRAWER LEGAL						
FILE / 3 DRAWER LETTER						
FILE / 3 DRAWER LEGAL						
FILE / 4 DRAWER LETTER						
FILE / 4 DRAWER LEGAL						
CONFERENCE TABLE / 36 X 60						
CONFERENCE TABLE / 60 X 60						
CONFERENCE TABLE / 48 ROUND						
CONFERENCE TABLE / 54 ROUND						
BOOKCASE						
STORAGE CABINET						
BLACKBOARD						
EASEL						
TELEPHONE / PRIVATE LINE						
CALCULATOR						
ADDING MACHINE						
DICTATING MACHINE						
PROJECTOR						
TOTAL						

reaching. Individual tasks are reduced, permitting more time for other kinds of work, in turn perhaps reducing overtime requirements and personnel projections. The volume of stored paper is decreased, lessening filing capacity and building-space needs.

The positive results of a paper-flow study of one network can trigger like studies of other networks. If so, the procedures are the same.

FURNITURE AND EQUIPMENT ANALYSIS

One of the basic aims of office landscaping is to provide functional furniture and equipment in a functional arrangement designed to serve the needs of the individual. The *furniture and equipment analysis* provides the general and specific criteria for the design and/or selection of furniture and equipment.

But, before the criteria for furniture and equipment arrangement can be established, an inventory of existing furniture and equipment must be conducted. This should include all individual workplaces, and group and special areas such as conference rooms, libraries, mail rooms, supply rooms, etc. The inventory should be complete, including items to be discarded, and should be compiled in the form of a chart, categorizing the quantities of each type of furniture and equipment under job level classifications taken from the chart of hierarchy and function.

While the inventory is being taken by the user group, a more detailed survey of a sample number of workplaces at all department levels can also be conducted by the working group. The purpose of the inventory is to list and categorize existing furniture and equipment, and the purpose of the sample survey is to investigate the use and misuse of these items. In a group of 200, a sampling of 50 is usually adequate.

The results of the survey can be summarized by outlining the discrepancies between what the furniture and equipment was designed for and how it is being used. For instance, desk tops and side tables might be used for storing file information, an indication of a lack or improper use of filing equipment. Desk drawers might contain stockpiled stationery items, an indication that an adequate departmental system is needed to

USER GROUP REPRESENTATIVES INVENTORY THEIR OWN TALLY GROUPS

MISUSE OF FURNITURE AND EQUIPMENT MAY INDICATE IMPROPER WORKPLACE DESIGN

SAMPLE SURVEY OF 50 TYPICAL WORKPLACES

ITEM	MACHINES	REFERENCE MATERIALS	PRINTOUT MATERIALS	IN/OUT BOX	DATA CARDS	PERSONAL ITEMS	OBSOLETE MATERIALS	SUPPLIES	STACKED PAPER	EMPTY	COMMENTS
	%	%	%	%	%	%	%	%	%	%	
DESK TOP	34	44		48	18				26		60 PERCENT OF WORKPLACES HAD ITEMS STORED ON DESK TOPS
DESK PEDESTAL						40					40 PERCENT USED PEDESTALS FOR OTHER THAN OFFICIAL PURPOSES
TABLE	22	37	30						22		100 PERCENT MISUSED TABLES
BOOKCASE		25	58		15	50		25	15		54 PERCENT MISUSED ONE OR MORE SHELVES
DESK RUNOFF	90	45		22				60			75 PERCENT MISUSED RUNOFFS
FILE CABINET		29	17			78	14	46	33	14	100 PERCENT PARTIALLY MISUSED — USUALLY BOTTOM DRAWER
CONFERENCE TABLE			50						50		100 PERCENT MISUSED FOR STORAGE
MACHINE TABLE	25	25	50							75	50 PERCENT MISUSED FOR STORAGE

dispense such items. An abundance of unused adding machines, typewriters, and other costly equipment might indicate a reduced need for these machines because of sharing.

If the misuse of furniture and equipment is substantial, it may be advantageous to represent the sample survey results in charts indicating the percentages of misuse.

NOTE: *It is a good idea to photograph the existing workplaces surveyed, if for no other reason than to make it possible to compare the final workplace with the original.*

As stated above, the purpose of the furniture and equipment analysis is to set forth general and specific criteria for a future furniture program. This program should be designed so that functional requirements prevail over grade entitlement, and it should facilitate and promote efficient work performance, allowing flexibility for job function changes.

Each specific criterion for the design and/or selection of furniture and furnishings should be categorized as *functional, environmental,* or *aesthetic,* and each criterion must be accompanied by an equally specific rationale. These detailed criteria are based on information from the furniture and equipment inventory, the results of the sample survey, and the knowledge of planning team members including specialists involved in the area.

All criteria for the furniture program must be reviewed by all members of the planning team and altered if necessary. This program sets the ground rules for future individual, group, and special workplace design.

Because of the number and complexity of specific furniture criteria, Section Four, "Furniture and Furnishings," is devoted to detailed descriptions of furniture requirements in the open landscape and to setting forth general and possible specific criteria.

FILING SYSTEM ANALYSIS

Certainly one of the most common ailments of businesses is the tendency to collect unnecessary file materials. Paper hoarding is usually the result of attempts by department personnel to gain status and importance

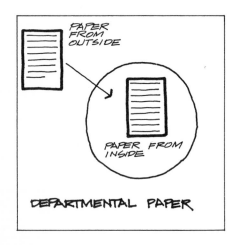

PAPER FROM OUTSIDE

PAPER FROM INSIDE

DEPARTMENTAL PAPER

SAMPLE FILES INVENTORY SHEET

NAME_____

TALLY GROUP NUMBER_____

FILE NAME/TITLE AND DOCUMENT TYPE	CODE	DOCUMENT SIZE	EXISTING TOTAL INCHES	TO BE AT WORKPLACE				TO BE IN GROUP FILE		TO BE IN CENTRAL FILE		OBSOLETE	REMARKS
				OPEN		CONFI-DENTIAL							
				P	G	P	G	P	G	P	G	O	

CODE

FL FOLDER / LOOSE
FF FOLDER / FASTENED
RB RING BINDER
BX BOXED
HB HARD BOUND
SB SOFT BOUND

CD CARDS
PO PRINTOUTS
OT OTHER / EXPLAIN

P PRESENT / EXISTING
G GROWTH / PROJECTED
O OBSOLETE / DESTROY

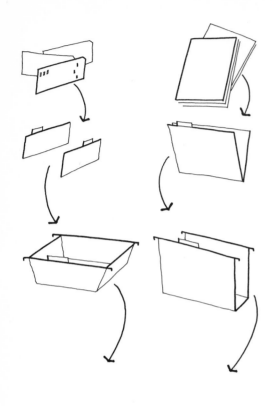

TECHNIQUE OF FILING
LOOSE MATERIALS

FILES
CARDS AND
GENERAL WORK PAPERS

TECHNIQUE OF FILING
BOUND MATERIALS

BOOKS
MANUALS AND REPORTS
MAGAZINES
AND PRINTOUTS

ACTIVE FILE STORAGE

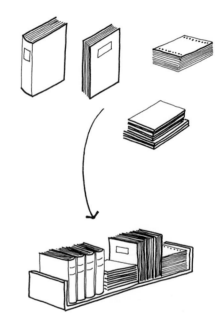

by amassing all sorts of records, such as files, cards, general work papers, books, manuals, reports, magazines, printouts, and stationery supplies. While an overabundance of file material may help satisfy a need for importance, its consequences are far-reaching: an individual can work with or handle just so much paper before it begins to erode work efficiency; hoarding documents creates retrieval problems for others requiring access to the information; and duplication of file material creates a storage problem that goes beyond the actual workplace of the hoarder. Frequent duplication of materials creates a need for more and more storage equipment, which occupies more and more building space, until the office becomes a warehouse for paper. Therefore, an efficient and continuing records-management program is of fundamental importance to a smoothly functioning task-oriented department.

The initial step in *filing system analysis* is to conduct a sample survey and an inventory of the present situation, similar to those in the furniture and equipment analysis. The inventory is most easily accomplished by means of a questionnaire to be completed by all department personnel, and the sample survey consists of spot checks by the planning team.

The design of the files inventory questionnaire varies with the nature of the department involved, but should include categorization of all types of file materials, measurement in inches of materials in each category, frequency of use evaluation, and notation of confidential and shared file materials. The inventory should gather data concerning materials not only at the individual's workplace, but also in any central or archive files which are under her/his jurisdiction.

The participation of the user group in the inventory is essential. These team members should provide assistance to departmental personnel by answering questions and helping with the measurements and assessments requested on the questionnaire.

While the users complete the inventory, members of the working group should conduct the sample survey to verify the information being recorded on the questionnaire. Like the furniture and equipment survey, the filing system survey's purpose is to define the use and misuse of file materials.

ORGANIZATIONS AVERAGE 21 FEET OF PAPER PER PERSON

PAPER HOARDING CAN TURN THE OFFICE INTO A WAREHOUSE FOR PAPER

WORKPLACE AVERAGE USABLE PAPER IS 2 FEET

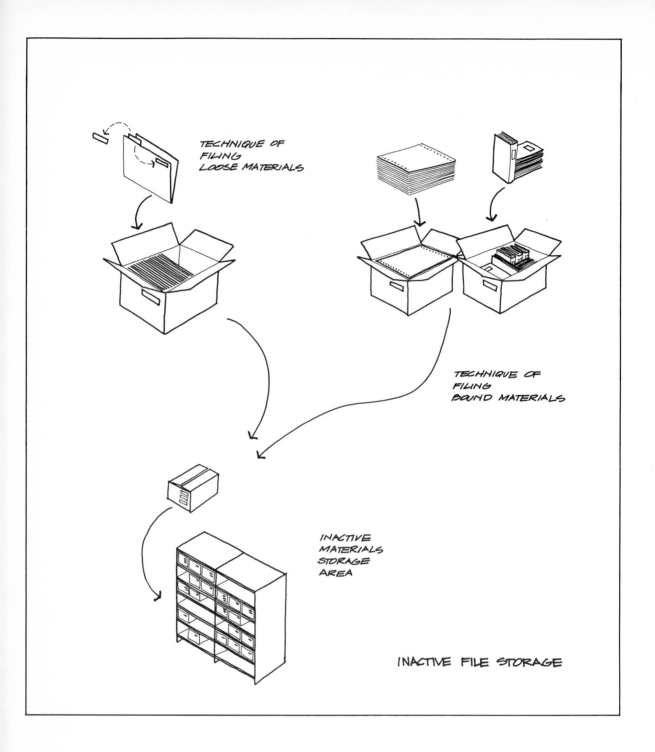

TECHNIQUE OF
FILING
LOOSE MATERIALS

TECHNIQUE OF
FILING
BOUND MATERIALS

INACTIVE
MATERIALS
STORAGE
AREA

INACTIVE FILE STORAGE

NOTE: *If scheduling allows, it is possible though not mandatory for the furniture and equipment, and filing system analyses to be conducted simultaneously in order to create as little interference with normal personnel tasks as possible.*

The filing system inventory and sample survey result in valuable planning information: file material categories, quantities of materials in these categories, intensity and scope of usage, and probability of duplication of material. These results can be compiled either by tally group or by the department as a whole and summarized in charts showing average file and reference material per person.

If the results of the inventory and survey indicate that a new filing system is needed, it should be carefully designed with the assistance of a filing consultant working as a specialist, and should suit the specific needs of the planned-for department in terms of file categories and mode of classification. There are many accepted classification systems, such as numerical, chronological, and alphabetical, and the one chosen for the department should meet the following criteria: the filing symbols should facilitate the search and location of materials—in other words, if an individual is most likely to recall material by subject, then filing symbols should reflect subjects; the symbols should be easy to remember; and, wherever feasible, the classification symbols should be standardized.

NOTE: *Symbols which relate directly to the classified materials are often the easiest to remember and to use. For example, "personnel" might be "Per"; "consumer price index," "CPI"; and so forth. Further, the standardization of symbols is necessary to permit materials usage by more than one person, whether files are generally shared or an employee is out of the office for a period of time and someone else must take over his/her tasks.*

The frequency of usage of materials within a department generally breaks down into *active, semiactive,* and *inactive* categories. Active files are used constantly by a given individual; semiactive files are used less frequently by a single employee, but are needed often and shared by a group; inactive materials are those used infrequently by anyone, and include legal or other documents altogether unused but necessary to

THE CLASSIFICATION SYSTEM SHOULD BE TAILORED TO THE DEPARTMENT

ACTIVE FILES   FOR INDIVIDUAL WORKPLACES

SEMIACTIVE FILES   SHARED WITHIN GROUP

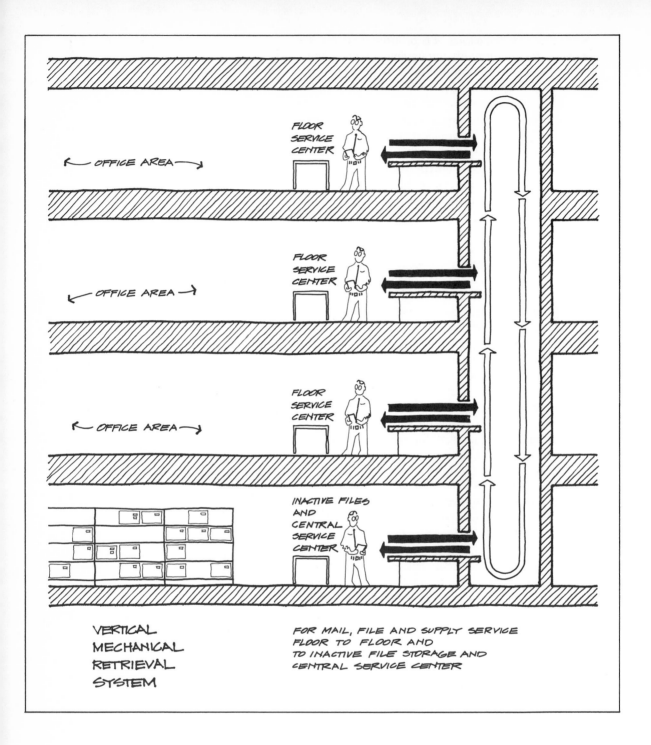

FLOOR SERVICE CENTER

← OFFICE AREA →

FLOOR SERVICE CENTER

← OFFICE AREA →

FLOOR SERVICE CENTER

← OFFICE AREA →

INACTIVE FILES AND CENTRAL SERVICE CENTER

VERTICAL MECHANICAL RETRIEVAL SYSTEM

FOR MAIL, FILE AND SUPPLY SERVICE FLOOR TO FLOOR AND TO INACTIVE FILE STORAGE AND CENTRAL SERVICE CENTER

maintain. The definition and scope of these categories may vary between planning projects, but the categories themselves are usually applicable.

Active files should be at the individual's workplace, readily available at any time. If several individuals are working with the same information, duplication is necessary. Semiactive files and records can be deposited with a group, giving members easy access to the material without the need for duplication. Inactive materials may be stored in less costly building space, such as the basement, if a retrieval system is included to afford fast access to the information.

NOTE: *There are several advantages to storing inactive files and records outside the main workplace area: more secure protection of the papers from fire or vandalism; less clutter around group work areas; and safer, more efficient workplaces with a minimum of files, books, and papers—fuel load in fire prevention language.*

A mechanical retrieval system may sound like a costly and slow means of handling paper; however, its cost is invariably more than offset by savings on prime office space. In addition, most mechanical retrieval systems supply the requested documents in ten minutes or less.

Whether the inactive materials storage area is in the basement, requiring a vertical conveyor retrieval system, or on the same floor as the department, requiring only an attendant, certain criteria must be met: an adequate transfer and retrieval procedure must be established in order to send and request particular documents; a cross referencing system must be developed which allows the location of specific materials by means of different kinds of information; confidential records must be available only to the proper individuals; and all systems and procedures must function together to allow the record storage attendant to locate any document, in or out of the storage area, at any time.

The *floor service center,* where department personnel send and receive documents, should have multiple functions in order to improve efficiency and minimize duplication of effort and equipment. It is the logical place for mail and message distribution, an ideal area for reproduction equipment and stationery

INACTIVE FILES ARE SELDOM USED BUT NECESSARY TO MAINTAIN

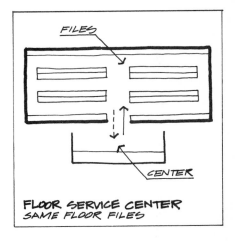

FLOOR SERVICE CENTER
SAME FLOOR FILES

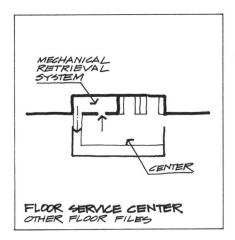

FLOOR SERVICE CENTER
OTHER FLOOR FILES

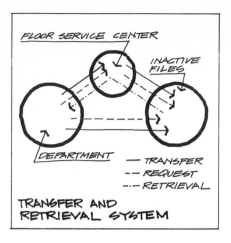

FLOOR SERVICE CENTER

INACTIVE FILES

DEPARTMENT

— TRANSFER
-- REQUEST
-·- RETRIEVAL

TRANSFER AND RETRIEVAL SYSTEM

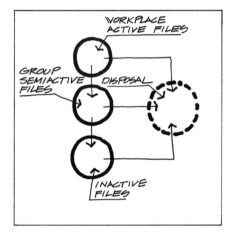

WORKPLACE ACTIVE FILES

GROUP SEMIACTIVE FILES

DISPOSAL

INACTIVE FILES

SPACE CALCULATION PRODUCES THE SQUARE FOOTAGE REQUIREMENTS OF ALL DEPARTMENTAL ELEMENTS

supply storage, and can, if properly located, serve as the floor's visitor reception center.

One of the most important considerations in developing an overall filing system is the disposal of materials. If paper is not systematically eliminated, it will increase to the point of choking the filing system. A disposal program is mandatory and must be effective at every level of file and records usage: the individual workplace, the group file station, and the inactive archive area. There is a tendency for individuals to feel they need old files at hand; however, many records are used once or twice and never referred to again. These materials, unless law requires their retention, should be discarded; even those which must be retained by law usually have a set life-span and should be destroyed when this has elapsed. Obviously, a few records may be needed indefinitely, but these are generally very few in number.

In most planning projects, the implementation of a new or revised filing system can begin before other planning tasks have been completed and the department moves into its new or renovated space. The disposal of unneeded files and records can be accomplished early in the planning with the positive results of increasing work efficiency and space by reducing existing quantities of paper. Other elements of the filing system can also be implemented provided this will neither create duplication of efforts at move-in, nor compromise the system before adequate filing equipment is available.

The results of the filing system analysis should produce not only criteria and procedures for filing, but also filing techniques, which in turn dictate the types of equipment needed. Although, in an actual office landscape planning project, the design and/or selection of equipment would interlock with the filing system analysis, it will be discussed in Section Four, ''Furniture and Furnishings.''

SPACE CALCULATION

Very early in the planning, usually during problem detection analysis, indicators begin to lead the planning team toward an office-layout type: conventional, with floor-to-ceiling partitions and closed office spaces;

open-plan; or some combination of the two. And most often, by the time the planning has progressed to *space calculation,* department personnel, as well as the planning team, have begun to have a feel for the most desirable layout type because of their ongoing involvement in and knowledge of planning activities. Though there is rarely, if *ever,* a unanimous opinion, there is usually a consensus in favor of a certain direction.

Nonetheless, it is advisable to develop a *layout option decision matrix.* It is possible to use several types of layouts as main categories, e.g., flexible open plan, fixed open plan, conventional plan, and combination open and conventional. However, it is much less confusing to use simply open- and conventional-plan headings. Any necessary combinations, such as conventional spaces in an open plan or vice versa, will still become apparent as the layout planning and design proceed.

If open and conventional plans are the two vertical matrix headings, the horizontal categories should list the criteria the final layout should fulfill, including: optimum communication, optimum co-use of group files, optimum workplace flexibility and rearrangement, optimum environment for all employee levels, and optimum departmental image. For each criterion, either a single layout heading can be selected as the better of the two, or each heading can be assigned a value from one to ten reflecting the degree to which it fulfills the given criterion. Then the values beneath each heading have only to be totaled to determine the layout type best suited to the planned-for department.

For the purposes of this book, and because several good explications of conventional space planning already exist, let us assume that the matrix of the sample department indicates an open plan should be followed.

The space calculation for an open-plan layout is a complex, detailed process. It is, however, necessary and valuable, producing the square footage requirements of any given departmental group, accurate for any configuration of open-plan layout.

NOTE: *One of the curious aspects of the open plan is that the total square footage determined for a particular project is stable, regardless of building configura-*

CRITERIA	CONVENTIONAL	OPEN PLAN
(criterion)		✓
(criterion)	✓	
(criterion)		✓
(criterion)		✓
(criterion)		✓
(criterion)		✓
(criterion)		✓
(criterion)	✓	
(criterion)		
(criterion)		✓
(criterion)		✓
TOTAL	2	8

LAYOUT OPTION DECISION MATRIX NUMBER

CRITERIA	CONVENTIONAL	OPEN PLAN
(criterion)	3	7
(criterion)	2	6
(criterion)	7	1
(criterion)		10
(criterion)	2	8
(criterion)	5	5
(criterion)	3	6
(criterion)	7	3
(criterion)	4	6
(criterion)	1	9
TOTAL	34	61

LAYOUT OPTION DECISION MATRIX VALUE

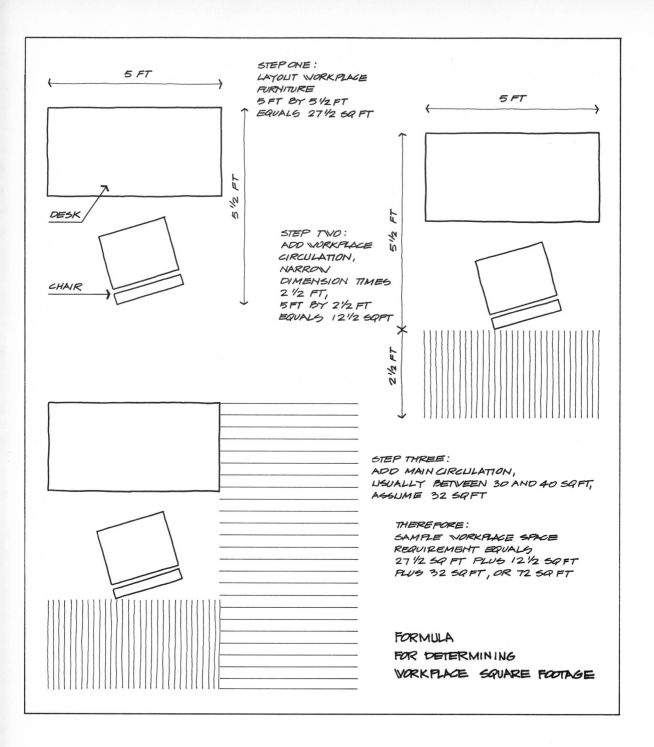

STEP ONE:
LAYOUT WORKPLACE
FURNITURE
5 FT BY 5½ FT
EQUALS 27½ SQ FT

5 FT

5½ FT

DESK

CHAIR

STEP TWO:
ADD WORKPLACE
CIRCULATION,
NARROW
DIMENSION TIMES
2½ FT,
5 FT BY 2½ FT
EQUALS 12½ SQ FT

5 FT

5½ FT

2½ FT

STEP THREE:
ADD MAIN CIRCULATION,
USUALLY BETWEEN 30 AND 40 SQ FT,
ASSUME 32 SQ FT

THEREFORE:
SAMPLE WORKPLACE SPACE
REQUIREMENT EQUALS
27½ SQ FT PLUS 12½ SQ FT
PLUS 32 SQ FT, OR 72 SQ FT

FORMULA
FOR DETERMINING
WORKPLACE SQUARE FOOTAGE

tion. This, of course, assumes the configuration is suitable for an open-plan layout (building configuration is discussed in Section Five, "The Facility"). On the other hand, the total square footage for any conventional plan varies, sometimes drastically, with different building configurations. The open-plan space does not change simply because it is not related to or affected by building modules and set corridor patterns.

Space calculation includes the development of *workplace standards* which are based on the information and conclusions drawn from the chart of hierarchy and function, work/time distribution matrix, furniture and equipment analysis, filing system analysis, and assessment of special requirements.

Individual workplaces are designed to suit the specific functions and needs of each user, including all aspects of her/his tasks and environment.

Group workplaces are designed for individuals sharing equipment and/or materials. These spaces can include conference areas, file and record facilities, reception areas, etc.

Special workplaces integral to the open plan must also be calculated and designed for such areas as wardrobes, lounges, floor service centers, multiple group conference areas, and so on. Other areas, such as central record storage spaces, cafeteria/dining facilities, recreation facilities, building reception spaces, and organization products display areas, are usually fixed conventional plans, and their space calculations may be derived in a conventional manner.

There is a formula for determining the space needed for each workplace type. It requires both mathematical and graphic computations, and includes the space needed for the workplace itself, circulation within the workplace, and main circulation.

First, the workplace is graphically laid out to scale, with each item of furniture and/or equipment placed logically and functionally. The sum of the square footages required for each item in this arrangement produces the work-station square footage. A simplistic example would be a desk, typically 2½ feet by 5 feet, plus 3 feet provided for a desk chair. This produces a workplace area 5½ feet by 5 feet, or 27½ square feet.

Second, the workplace circulation is found by multiplying the narrow dimension of the workplace by a

> WORKPLACE STANDARDS ARE DEVELOPED FOR INDIVIDUAL, GROUP, AND SPECIAL WORKPLACES

> WORKPLACE SQUARE FOOTAGE
> =
> FURNITURE
> +
> WORKPLACE CIRCULATION
> +
> MAIN CIRCULATION

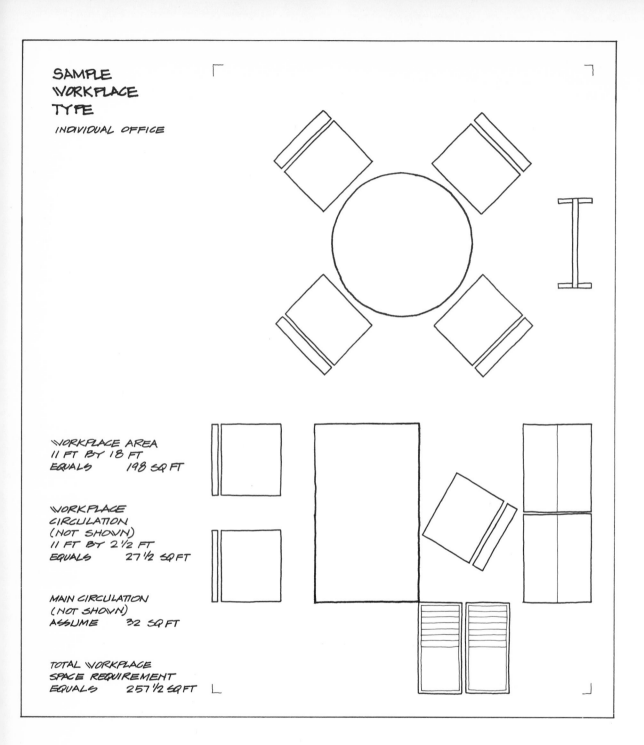

SAMPLE
WORKPLACE
TYPE
INDIVIDUAL OFFICE

WORKPLACE AREA
11 FT BY 18 FT
EQUALS   198 SQ FT

WORKPLACE
CIRCULATION
(NOT SHOWN)
11 FT BY 2 1/2 FT
EQUALS   27 1/2 SQ FT

MAIN CIRCULATION
(NOT SHOWN)
ASSUME   32 SQ FT

TOTAL WORKPLACE
SPACE REQUIREMENT
EQUALS   257 1/2 SQ FT

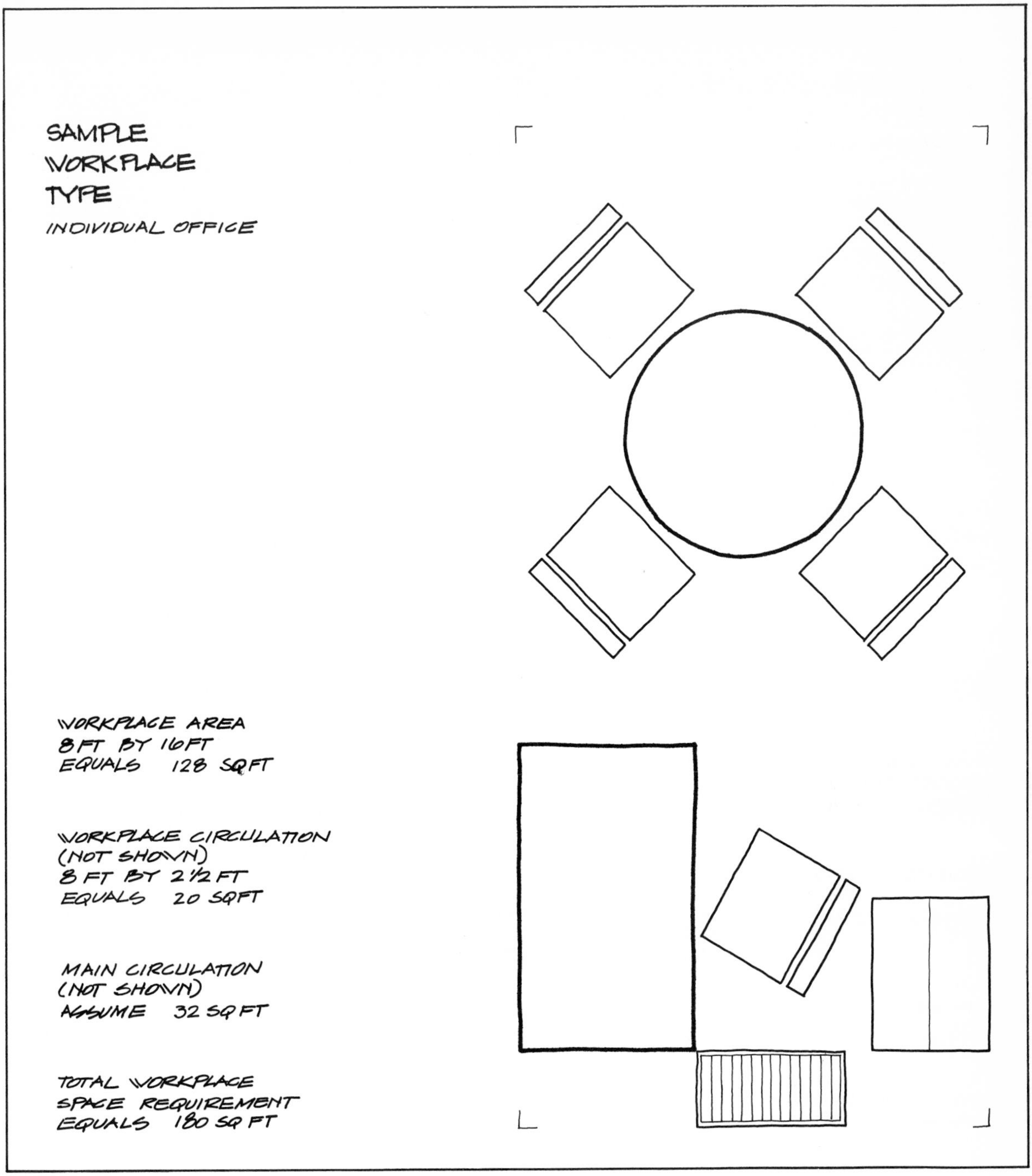

SAMPLE
WORKPLACE
TYPE
INDIVIDUAL OFFICE

WORKPLACE AREA
8 FT BY 16 FT
EQUALS   128 SQ FT

WORKPLACE CIRCULATION
(NOT SHOWN)
8 FT BY 2½ FT
EQUALS   20 SQ FT

MAIN CIRCULATION
(NOT SHOWN)
ASSUME   32 SQ FT

TOTAL WORKPLACE
SPACE REQUIREMENT
EQUALS   180 SQ FT

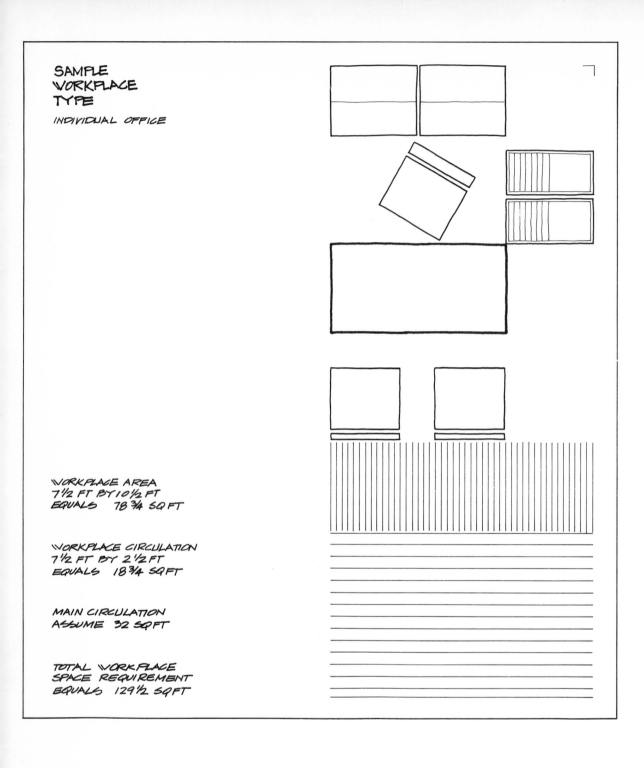

SAMPLE
WORKPLACE
TYPE

INDIVIDUAL OFFICE

WORKPLACE AREA
7½ FT BY 10½ FT
EQUALS   78¾ SQ FT

WORKPLACE CIRCULATION
7½ FT BY 2½ FT
EQUALS   18¾ SQ FT

MAIN CIRCULATION
ASSUME 32 SQ FT

TOTAL WORKPLACE
SPACE REQUIREMENT
EQUALS   129½ SQ FT

SAMPLE
WORKPLACE
TYPE
INDIVIDUAL OFFICE

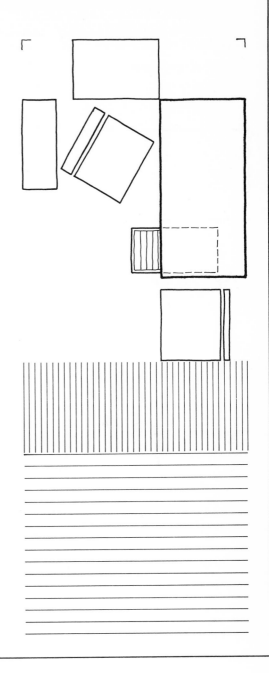

WORKPLACE AREA
6½ FT BY 9 FT
EQUALS   58½ SQ FT

WORKPLACE CIRCULATION
6½ FT BY 2½ FT
EQUALS   16¼ SQ FT

MAIN CIRCULATION
ASSUME   32 SQ FT

TOTAL WORKPLACE
SPACE REQUIREMENT
EQUALS   106¾ SQ FT

SAMPLE
WORKPLACE
TYPE

INDIVIDUAL OFFICES

WORKPLACE AREA
5½ FT BY 7½ FT
EQUALS 41½ SQ FT

WORKPLACE CIRCULATION
5½ FT BY 2½ FT
EQUALS 13¾ SQ FT

MAIN CIRCULATION
ASSUME 32 SQ FT

TOTAL WORKPLACE
SPACE REQUIREMENT
EQUALS 87 SQ FT

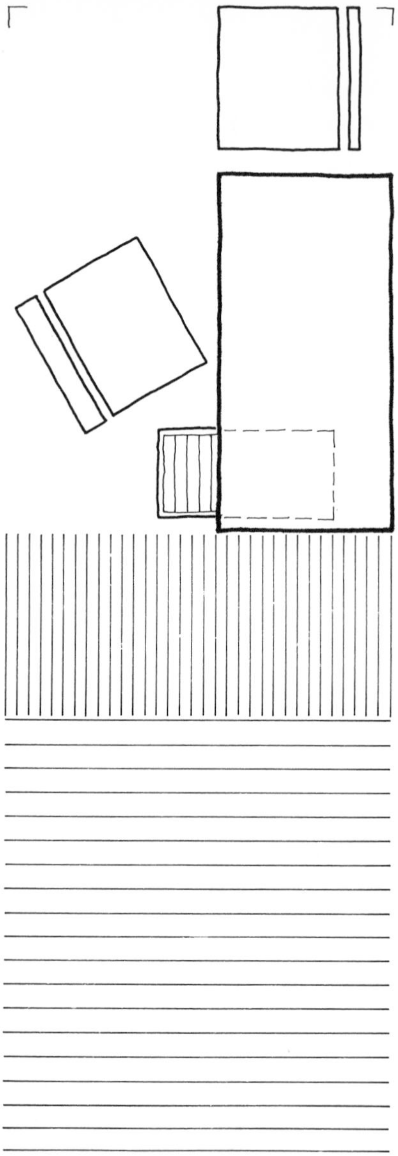

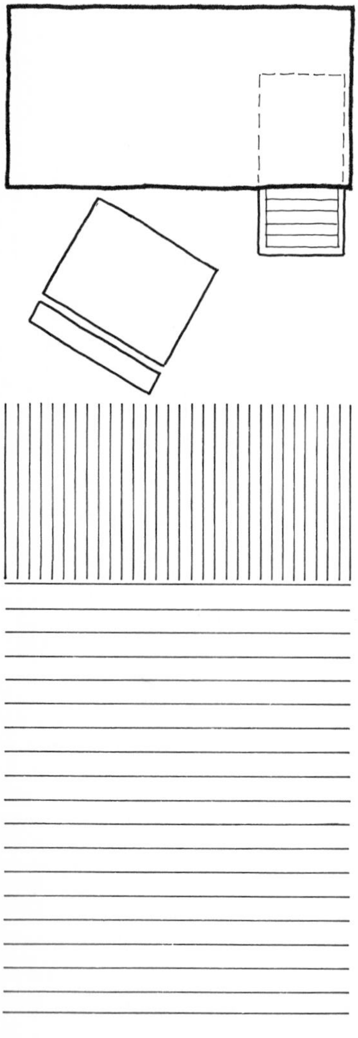

WORKPLACE AREA
5 FT BY 5½ FT
EQUALS 27½ SQ FT

WORKPLACE
CIRCULATION
5 FT BY 2½ FT
EQUALS 12½ SQ FT

MAIN CIRCULATION
ASSUME 32 SQ FT

TOTAL WORKPLACE
SPACE REQUIREMENT
EQUALS 72 SQ FT

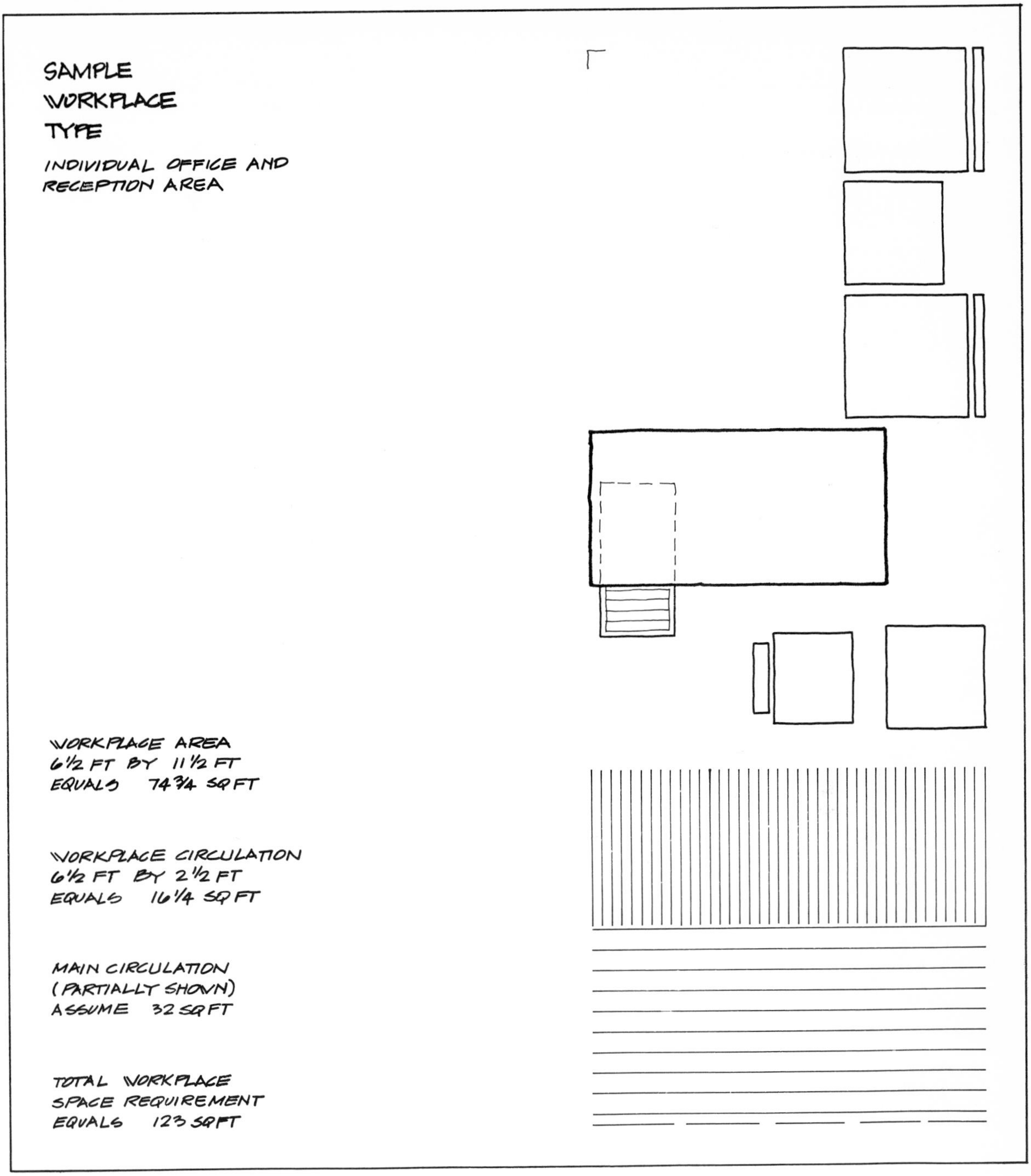

SAMPLE
WORKPLACE
TYPE

INDIVIDUAL OFFICE AND
RECEPTION AREA

WORKPLACE AREA
6½ FT BY 11½ FT
EQUALS 74¾ SQ FT

WORKPLACE CIRCULATION
6½ FT BY 2½ FT
EQUALS 16¼ SQ FT

MAIN CIRCULATION
(PARTIALLY SHOWN)
ASSUME 32 SQ FT

TOTAL WORKPLACE
SPACE REQUIREMENT
EQUALS 123 SQ FT

SAMPLE
WORKPLACE
TYPE
GROUP CONFERENCE AREA

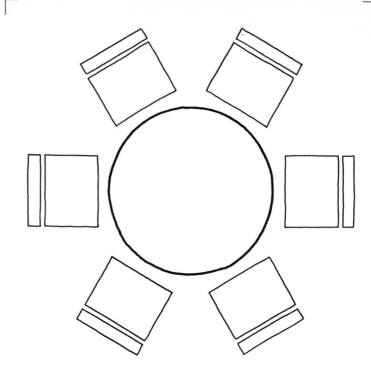

WORKPLACE AREA
10½ FT BY 11½ FT
EQUALS   120¾ SQ FT

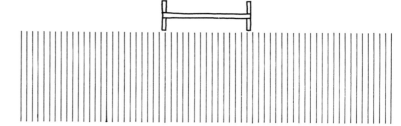

WORKPLACE CIRCULATION
10½ FT BY 2½ FT
EQUALS   26¼ SQ FT

MAIN CIRCULATION
NOT INCLUDED IN
SPACE CALCULATION FORMULA

TOTAL WORKPLACE
SPACE REQUIREMENT
EQUALS   147 SQ FT

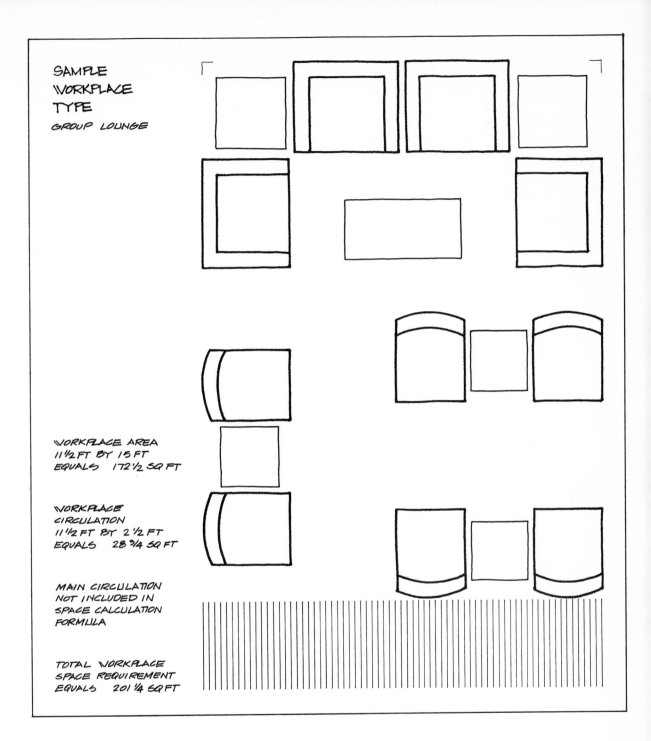

SAMPLE
WORKPLACE
TYPE
GROUP LOUNGE

WORKPLACE AREA
11½ FT BY 15 FT
EQUALS   172½ SQ FT

WORKPLACE
CIRCULATION
11½ FT BY 2½ FT
EQUALS   28¾ SQ FT

MAIN CIRCULATION
NOT INCLUDED IN
SPACE CALCULATION
FORMULA

TOTAL WORKPLACE
SPACE REQUIREMENT
EQUALS   201¼ SQ FT

SAMPLE GROUP SPACE CALCULATION SHEET

TALLY GROUP NUMBER _____
NUMBER OF PERSONS _____

INDIVIDUAL WORKPLACE CALCULATIONS

JOB TITLE, NAME OR CODE	WORKPLACE TYPE	NUMBER	SQ FT EACH	TOTAL SQ FT
J. NOBLES	A	1	257.75	257.75
ADMIN. ASST.	C	2	129.50	259.00
R/A	G	1	123.00	123.00
C/B	D	6	106.75	640.50
S/A	E	3	72.00	216.00
TOTAL/INDIVIDUAL WORKPLACE REQUIREMENTS				1496.25

GROUP OR SHARED WORKPLACE CALCULATIONS

DESCRIPTION	WORKPLACE TYPE	NUMBER	SQ FT EACH	TOTAL SQ FT
CONFERENCE	J	1	147.00	147.00
GROUP FILE	L	1	25.00	25.00
TOTAL/GROUP WORKPLACE REQUIREMENTS				172.00
TOTAL/GROUP SPACE REQUIREMENTS				1668.25

factor of 2½ feet. In the example on page 67, the narrow dimension is 5 feet; therefore the workplace circulation would be 12½ square feet.

Third, the main circulation is added to workplace and workplace-circulation square footages. It is a set figure, consistent in all the workplaces in the project. First-time planners frequently tend to assign more square footage to main circulation than is really necessary; and though it does vary between projects, experience shows that the main circulation figure is usually between 30 and 40 square feet, depending on the spaciousness desired by the department and the planning team. For the example, assume 32 square feet; this workplace type, then, requires 72 square feet of space.

After all the workplace types are measured, the required square footage for tally groups can be computed. This can be accomplished easily by using a *group space calculation work sheet,* which includes the required space for each individual, as well as the required spaces for group workplace types. If group expansion is anticipated in the near future, projections should be included as vacant workplaces.

The group space calculation work sheet lists workplace types and their required square footages by job titles, with the number of persons for any given position shown alongside the appropriate job title. By multiplying the number of people in each position by the workplace square footage each one requires, a total square footage per job title can be achieved, and the sum of these gives the total square footage needed for individual workplace types. The group space calculation work sheet also lists group workplace types, and the number and space requirements of each. The sum of these square footages can then be added to that of individual workplace types to find the total space required by the group.

A *special workplace calculation* must also be undertaken. This is a simple listing of those special areas not assigned to any tally group. Usually these are few in number because most special areas are used more intensively by one group than any other, and are therefore included in that group's square footage calculation. However, space calculations for unassigned

GROUP SPACE CALCULATION SHOULD INCLUDE PROJECTED EXPANSION

SPECIAL WORKPLACES ARE THOSE AREAS NOT ASSIGNED ANY PARTICULAR TALLY GROUP

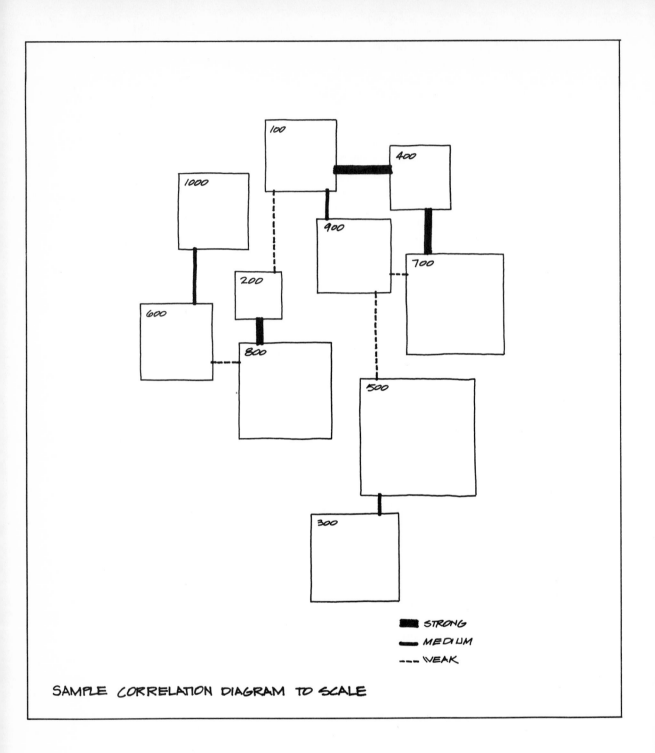

100

400

1000

900

200

700

600

800

500

300

STRONG
MEDIUM
---- WEAK

SAMPLE CORRELATION DIAGRAM TO SCALE

SAMPLE TALLY GROUP INTRA-ACTION SHEET

TALLY GROUP NUMBER _____
NUMBER OF PERSONS _____
TOTAL SQUARE FEET _____

INDIVIDUAL	INTRA-ACTION	WORKPLACE	GROUP WORKPLACE	SPECIAL
T. ALLEN				TELEPHONE
C. SACKREY				TELEPHONE
J. MILLER				TELEPHONE
H. STEPHENS				TELEPHONE AND ELECTRICAL
C. HANZLICEK				TELEPHONE (CONTROL) AND ELECTRICAL
FUTURE WORKPLACE				ELECTRICAL

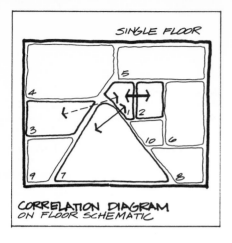

SINGLE FLOOR

CORRELATION DIAGRAM
ON FLOOR SCHEMATIC

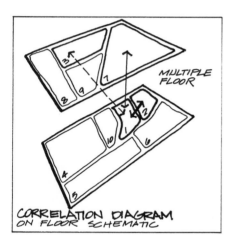

MULTIPLE FLOOR

CORRELATION DIAGRAM
ON FLOOR SCHEMATIC

special work areas should be computed as group areas are.

The total square footage required for the department is merely the sum of the individual, group, and special workplace square footages.

After all workplace standards and space requirements have been calculated, they should be applied to the correlation diagram developed earlier in the planning. The initial diagram presented all tally groups as the same size, and should be altered at this point to reflect the established square footages of these groups. In addition, special workplaces and their required square footages should be added to the diagram. In other words, the correlation diagram should now be drawn to scale and include all the major elements of the department. Individual workplaces should not yet be incorporated.

In an actual planning project, specialists would have been evaluating site limitations and alternative building designs concurrently with the planning activities discussed so far, and could indicate possible square footages per floor. It may be desirable to construct a three-dimensional correlation diagram if more than one building floor is required to house the department. This diagram can be used to determine which tally groups may be located on different floors without major communication interruptions.

Though the correlation diagram may have to be altered to accord with the building design, it should not be compromised hastily. Any alteration of the correlation diagram interferes with optimum communication, and a major alteration greatly impairs communication and work-flow efficiency.

Tally group intra-actions must also be established as a guide to the open-plan designer, although the final layout of the department cannot be accomplished until furniture and equipment have been selected and/or designed and the facility design has progressed further (see Sections Four and Five). Up to this point, there has been no endeavor to assess ideal communication lines and work-flow processes within tally groups. The communication analysis pertained only to interactions between groups, not communication within them.

The assessment of group intra-actions is relatively easy, and should be done by the group itself. A *tally*

SAMPLE TALLY SHEET

FOR THE SMALL ORGANIZATION

NAME _____

TITLE OR CODE _____

INSIDE CONTACTS

INDIVIDUAL	CODE	TELEPHONE CALLS RECEIVED	TOTAL	PAPERS RECEIVED	TOTAL	VISITS AND/OR CONFERENCES	TOTAL
L. STEPHENS	01						
J.H. ALLEN	02						
P. SACKRET	03						
C. WOHLER	04						
M. McGUIRE	05						
S. THON	06						
P. EVERWINE	07						
S. STARKMAN	08						
M. RISCH	09						
E. EVETT	10						

OUTSIDE CONTACTS

CONTACT	CODE	CONTACTS RECEIVED			CONTACTS MADE		
		TELEPHONE	PAPER	VISITS CONF.	TELEPHONE	PAPER	VISITS CONF.
WAREHOUSE	100						
OTHER							
OTHER							
OTHER							

group intra-action sheet should be provided for this purpose by the planning team. It should include a list of the group's individuals by name and job title, a small-scale drawing of each individual's workplace and any group equipment he/she uses intensively, and special requirements such as telephone, signal, or electrical service. Group members should assign values to their interactions with other members by means of heavy or double lines for strong interaction, single for medium, and dotted for light, just as in the correlation diagram. The information on each group's intra-action sheet is used in determining the optimum arrangement of individual workplaces within that group's area.

PLANNING FOR THE SMALL ORGANIZATION

Planning for the small organization, say up to 150 people, is essentially the same as planning for the medium-sized organization discussed in the bulk of this section, except that it is more streamlined. The same activities are included, but usually do not require as much time overall.

The planning team may be smaller with probably no more than three people on the working group, two or three on the review and decision committee, and no user group representatives. Chances are the specialists can remain about the same.

The user group may be omitted simply because communication between the planning team and all members of the organization is complete without the necessity of representatives. In planning for a small organization, it is also easier to tally communications individually than by tally groups.

In addition, less formal means of information gathering are advisable, emphasizing personal interviews over questionnaires. The information documented can also be presented less formally.

PLANNING FOR THE LARGE ORGANIZATION

There are usually no fundamental changes in planning structure and activities when applied to a large organi-

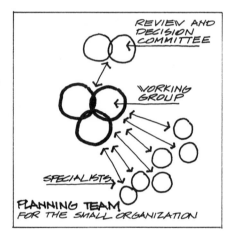

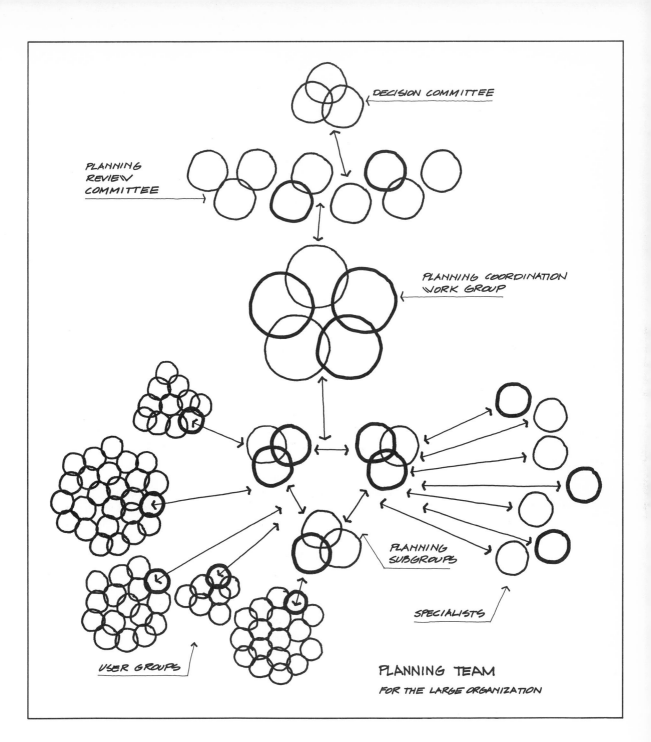

DECISION COMMITTEE

PLANNING REVIEW COMMITTEE

PLANNING COORDINATION WORK GROUP

PLANNING SUBGROUPS

SPECIALISTS

USER GROUPS

PLANNING TEAM
FOR THE LARGE ORGANIZATION

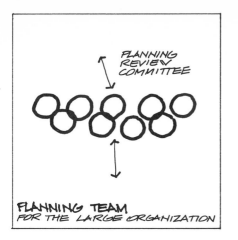

PLANNING TEAM
FOR THE LARGE ORGANIZATION

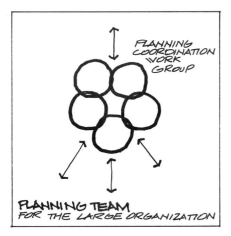

PLANNING TEAM
FOR THE LARGE ORGANIZATION

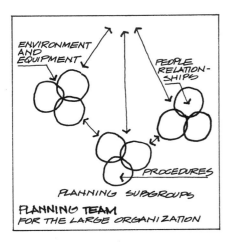

PLANNING SUBGROUPS
PLANNING TEAM
FOR THE LARGE ORGANIZATION

zation, unless the project involves several thousand employees. In this case one of the major changes is in the planning team. An overlapping structure must be established, consisting of a decision committee, a planning review committee, a planning coordination work group, three planning subgroups, and user groups and specialists as required.

The decision committee should consist of approximately three top-management personnel, and is responsible for making final decisions concerning expenditures, acceptance of proposals, recommended actions, and the like.

The planning review committee should be composed of one or two people from each division or department within the organization. This committee is responsible for formulating planning policies and directions.

The planning coordination work group should have about five members, and is similar to the working group described previously in this section. It is responsible for accomplishing the initial planning steps in the project and coordinating the activities of the three planning subgroups.

The subgroups vary in size, each structured around one of the four basic elements of the organization, discussed in Section Two, "Complexity of Planning." The fourth element, products, is covered generally by all the subgroups.

One subgroup is responsible for environment and equipment, and should establish criteria for the physical aspects of the office environment, such as air conditioning, lighting, acoustics, etc.; determine the space-management program; establish criteria for furniture and equipment; and prepare architectural, interior design, and aesthetic criteria for the project.

Another subgroup's tasks concern procedures, such as communication analyses, filing system analyses, and paper-flow studies.

The third subgroup deals with people relationships, including preparing and analyzing employee-attitude surveys; educating and preparing employees for changes in organizational structure and environment; and analyzing hierarchical structure, job functions, work/time distribution, status symbols, and centralization versus decentralization of activities.

Planning for very large organizations also requires the use of computers. Although this would be costly and inefficient for small or medium-sized organizations, it is necessary in large projects in order to process the greater bulk of planning data.

Often, large organizations can be planned for department by department in a fashion similar to medium-sized organizations; however, projects involving very complex organizational structures, such as large buildings, building complexes, hospitals, universities, cities, or new towns, should be planned for comprehensively from the beginning.

Furniture and Furnishings

Within the context of open-plan office landscaping, *furniture and furnishings* are defined as the movable elements of the physical environment (fixed environmental elements will be discussed in Section Five, "The Facility"), and include the typical items of furniture in an office: desks, credenzas, chairs, files, etc.; and certain items unique to open planning, such as screens, planters, and wardrobes.

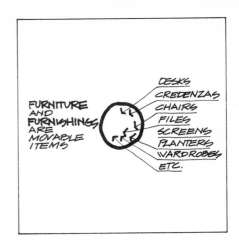

While furniture and furnishings typically found in both conventional offices and open-plan landscapes, for instance desks, may appear to be similar, they are selected on the basis of different criteria. Generally, a number of desks which provide writing surfaces, file pedestals, drawers, and skirts on three sides are suitable for conventional offices. Whether the desks are made of wood, metal, fiber glass, or some combination of these, makes little difference. Usually cost, appearance, standardization, and status are the main determinants, for any of these desks will work equally well in enclosed, conventional offices housing one or two persons. However, in open landscapes, other selection criteria must be considered. The desks must not only fulfill normal functional requirements for writing, reading, paper processing, telephoning, and so on, but must also be considered in light of arrangement flexibility, acoustics, and aesthetic performance in areas with many people and furnishings.

Consequently, in any given open-plan office landscape project, furniture, furnishings, and equipment must be considered individually and tested against criteria established by the planning team.

The following general criteria for furniture and furnishings should be considered before any specific criteria are established:

■ Each item should serve one general purpose only; that is, two basic functions, such as writing and filing, should not be combined in a single item of furniture—a desk with file space.

■ Acoustics are critical, and acoustical evaluation of materials, surfaces, and panels, especially vertical panels such as desk skirts, is absolutely necessary.

■ For maximum flexibility, each item of furniture should be easily movable without special tools.

■ Work surfaces should be light-colored, with matte finishes to aid work tasks—dark, shiny desk surfaces

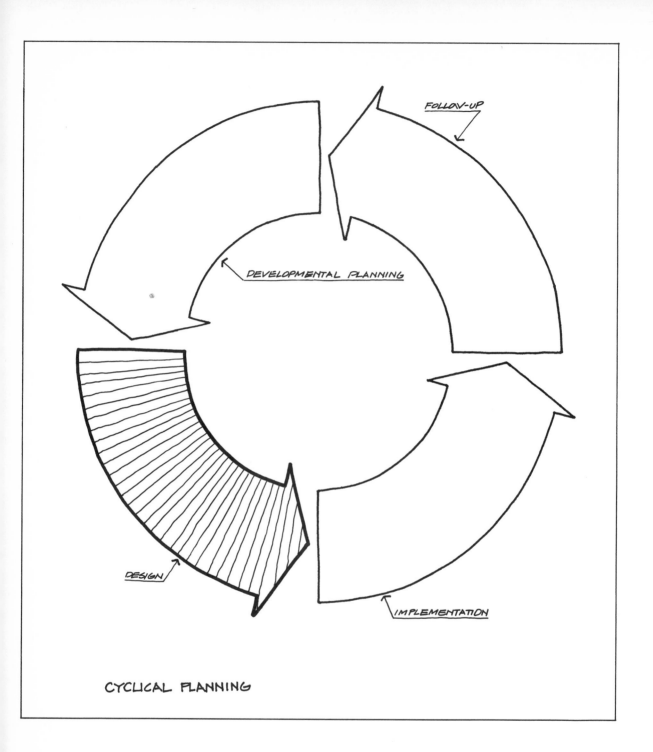

FOLLOW-UP

DEVELOPMENTAL PLANNING

IMPLEMENTATION

DESIGN

CYCLICAL PLANNING

PSYCHOLOGICAL "SPACE EATER"

PSYCHOLOGICAL "SPACE MAKER"

FURNITURE SHOULD BE TRANSPARENT

cause glare and are incompatible with normal off-white work papers.

- Furniture should be transparent, or open—heavy-looking, skirted furniture reflects sound and causes work areas to seem crowded.
- Each piece of furniture should meet the particular requirements of the user and department.
- Furniture design and/or selection should never be preconceived.

NOTE: *Approaching furniture design and/or selection without preconceived solutions should be emphasized. Too often, organizations planning open landscapes review furniture manufacturers' products and try to determine which line they want in their new spaces before establishing their own furniture criteria.*

SPECIFIC CRITERIA DEVELOPMENT

In analyzing and evaluating workplace needs, the planning team should set forth specific criteria for the design and/or selection of furniture and furnishings, as described in Section Three, "Furniture and Equipment Analysis." Each criterion should be supported by a written rationale and categorized as functional, environmental, or aesthetic. The planning team should establish the criteria, place them individually on index cards for display in the planning room, and arrange, alter, expand, eliminate, and review them until a consensus is reached. It is sometimes helpful to list the criteria in order of importance under the above three categories.

Without a doubt, there are excellent open-plan furniture systems. Although some deviate from the basic criterion that each item should be for one purpose only, these systems have been successfully used in many projects. But before thinking about any particular system or piece of furniture, the office landscape planner must understand the fundamental requirements for open-plan furniture and furnishings. Once these are understood, systems, as well as individual items, can be evaluated more successfully.

Desk   The desk, sometimes referred to as a standard office table, is the basic unit of most workplaces, and is

STANDARD DESK

PLAN

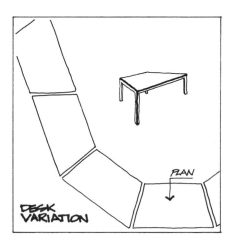

DESK VARIATION

PLAN

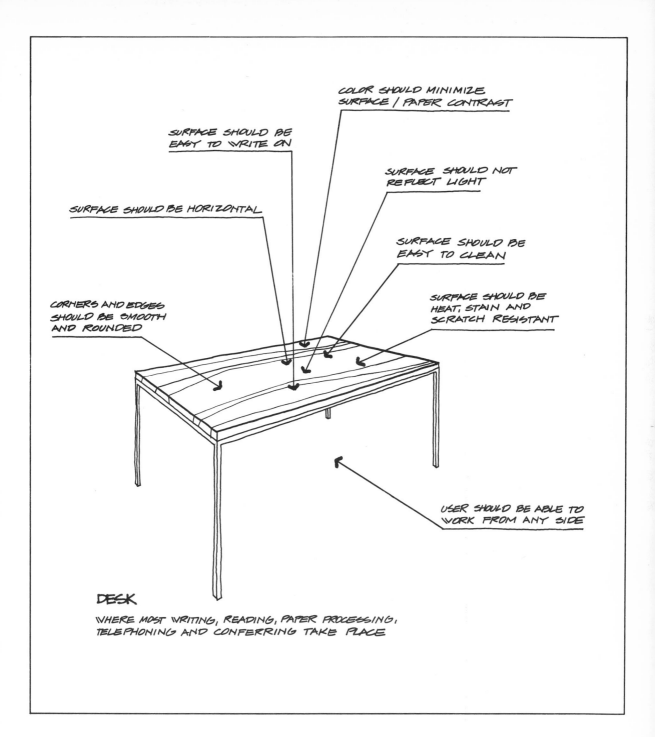

COLOR SHOULD MINIMIZE
SURFACE / PAPER CONTRAST

SURFACE SHOULD BE
EASY TO WRITE ON

SURFACE SHOULD NOT
REFLECT LIGHT

SURFACE SHOULD BE HORIZONTAL

SURFACE SHOULD BE
EASY TO CLEAN

CORNERS AND EDGES
SHOULD BE SMOOTH
AND ROUNDED

SURFACE SHOULD BE
HEAT, STAIN AND
SCRATCH RESISTANT

USER SHOULD BE ABLE TO
WORK FROM ANY SIDE

DESK

WHERE MOST WRITING, READING, PAPER PROCESSING,
TELEPHONING AND CONFERRING TAKE PLACE

where the bulk of writing, reading, paper processing, telephoning, and conferring occurs. Its size should comfortably permit usage at all workplaces and allow the average person to reach papers and equipment on its surface from a central working position. It should also have enough clearance to permit the user to work in a seated position from any side and to roll an individual file cart under the desk. The surface should be horizontal, flat, easy to write on and to clean. It should be heat, stain, and scratch resistant, with smooth, rounded edges for safety. Its color should minimize surface/paper contrast, and its finish should not reflect window or ceiling light. In addition, the desk should have runners for a utility drawer which can be moved from the left to the right side by hand, and an attachable modesty panel if one is needed.

Typing Table   This unit is normally provided in workplaces where a substantial portion of time, say 30 percent or more, is devoted to typing. The typing table should be a self-contained unit, large enough to support a typewriter and related material, and should include a shallow drawer for onionskin, carbon paper, and other supplies too flimsy to store vertically in a file cart. For flexibility, the drawer should be interchangeable from left to right. The typing table's surface, finish, and so forth, should meet the same criteria as the desk unit.

Machine Table   The machine table is similar to the typing table, but smaller, and is included in workplaces where adding and calculating machines are required, or where typewriters are needed less than 30 percent of the time. It is an ideal unit for shared equipment and should have glides or casters to permit easy relocation. The machine table should also meet the surface criteria set forth for the desk.

Conference Table   The conference table should be suitable for meetings of four to six people. A round conference table is requisite so that the users may sit at any point around the table and communicate easily and equally. Again, other criteria are similar to those for the desk unit.

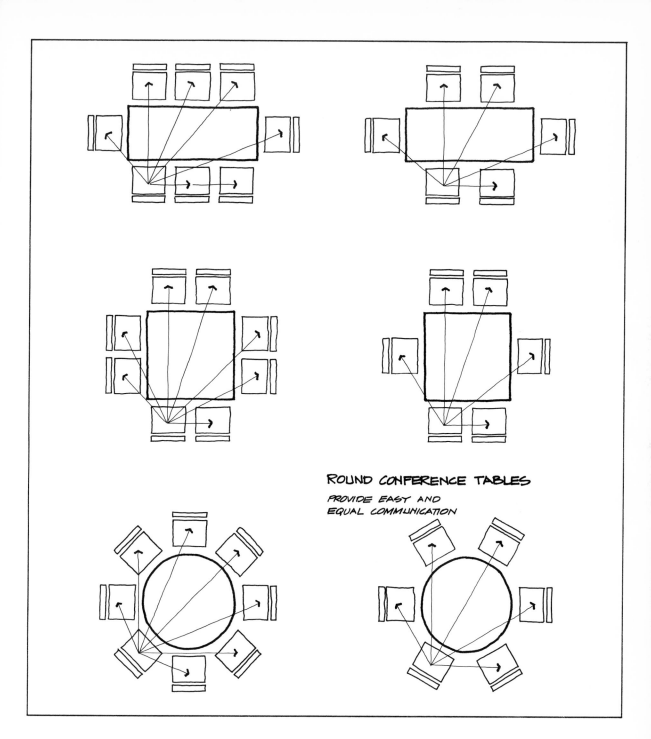

ROUND CONFERENCE TABLES

PROVIDE EASY AND
EQUAL COMMUNICATION

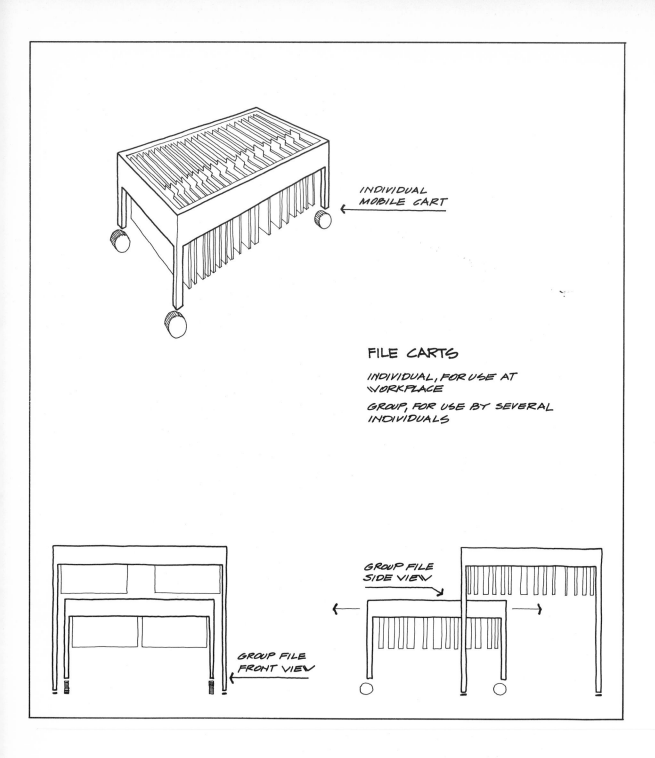

INDIVIDUAL
MOBILE CART

FILE CARTS

INDIVIDUAL, FOR USE AT
WORKPLACE

GROUP, FOR USE BY SEVERAL
INDIVIDUALS

GROUP FILE
SIDE VIEW

GROUP FILE
FRONT VIEW

File Cart   The cart is used to store active files and general work papers at the workplace. The unit should be designed for suspended file folders, and should accommodate letter- and legal-size paper, and computer printouts. The cart can be either open or closed on the sides; however, the bottom should be open to permit easy retrieval of misfiled papers. It must be rigid, but lightweight, with casters designed to roll easily on carpet. The main body of the unit should be off the floor for easy cleaning, yet low enough to roll under the utility drawer of a desk. It is essential that the cart be designed with smooth, rounded edges for the safety of users, clothing, and furniture and equipment.

Some office landscape projects require workplace storage of active confidential materials in enclosed, lockable file carts. However, these closed carts should be kept to a minimum because an increase in flat surface areas may cause acoustical problems.

NOTE: *In many instances, confidential and semiconfidential files are more secure if no attention is brought to them by notation, stamps, tags, and/or special equipment. This is true in both conventional and open-landscape areas.*

Group File   This unit is for storage of active and semi-active files, and general work papers, shared by and deposited with a group. The group file unit is similar to the individual file cart, but larger. It usually consists of two elements, each twice as large as an individual cart: a semifixed unit for working in a standing position, and a lower unit which rolls under the semifixed unit and is designed for working in a seated position.

Because group files are seldom at any individual's workplace, each level of the unit should have a work surface for sorting, searching, and filing papers. These surfaces should have the same characteristics as those of the desk, and must be movable to permit easy access to all files.

The group file unit provides considerable flexibility not only by freeing the individual workplace of excess paper, but also by accommodating various storage needs through the use of the upper unit only, both upper and lower units, or several complete units side by side.

CLOSED FILE CART

PLAN

CF

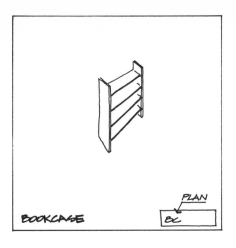

BOOKCASE   PLAN
                           BC

BOOKCASE
WITH CREDENZA   PLAN
                           BCC

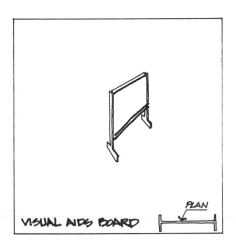

VISUAL AIDS BOARD   PLAN

Bookcase The bookcase is for storage of active bound materials, such as books, manuals, magazines, and reports. Although it can also be used as supplemental storage for active files, general work papers, and computer printouts, this should be resricted to short-term tasks requiring extraordinary quantities of materials. The bookcase is not intended to replace the file cart.

The unit should be designed with interchangeable shelves, including tilted ones with edgelips for storage of soft-cover materials. It can also be designed with open double-depth shelves to permit use from either side. Because one double unit costs considerably less than two single units, this saves money as well as space.

The height of the bookcase may vary, but should not extend above visual/acoustical screens or visual aids boards. It should also have adequate floor clearance for cleaning. The unit must be stable, with a minimum of racking, and, at the same time, lightweight.

In addition to the shelves, the bookcase may have an optional file unit, similar to a credenza. Though this option is costly, it may be necessary for storage of dictation equipment, minicalculators, and confidential files. In a workplace which requires a bookcase unit and a lockable file cart, it is often advantageous to eliminate the cart and add the file unit to the bookcase. The considerations for safety and construction should be similar to those for the furniture described above.

Visual Aids Board This unit serves as a chalkboard, tack board, easel, and bulletin board, and is used in conference areas and those workplaces which require conference facilities. The visual aids board should be designed for the user to work in a standing position, and generally has a chalkboard on one side and a tack board on the other. It must be stable and lightweight and must have carpet glides for maneuverability. In addition to the vertical boards, the unit should have a tray for chalk, pins, felt-tip markers, etc. The tray should be at a comfortable height and have an edgelip for supporting illustration boards and the like. Across the top of the unit, adjustable pegs or clamps should be provided for hanging paper pads, grid paper, and other items that are not self-supporting.

NOTE: *In some instances, visual aids boards are designed to include projection screens for slides, movies, overhead projectors, etc.; however, such requirements are seldom justified by needs. Experience has shown that, in most organizations, visual aids boards are working tools for small conferences; when presentations requiring projection equipment are made, larger groups of people are usually involved, and the conferences are more formal. Consequently, special conference facilities are recommended over complicated visual aids boards.*

Chairs Generally an open-landscape project requires three kinds of chairs. The first is a typical desk chair to be used for reading, writing, paper processing, telephoning, and holding conferences at the workplace desk. This chair should swivel, roll easily on carpet, and have adjustable seat height and tilt tension. It should also be designed to permit the addition or removal of arms.

The second is a standard machine chair to be used at workplaces where the majority of tasks involve typewriters, calculators, adding machines, and the like. In addition to the characteristics required for the desk chair, the machine chair should have adjustable back height and back-support tension. In all cases, adjustments should be easily accomplished without special tools.

The third chair is for conference and reception areas, and workplace desk sides. The requirements for this chair are not as stringent as for the desk and machine units because it is not used full time. However, chairs used for conferences should have tilt/swivel capabilities. In all cases, safety for individuals and, because the chairs are frequently moved, safety for furnishings must be considered.

Special seating units, such as drafting stools, dining chairs, and library and lounge furniture may also be needed. However, because these are special furnishings, each department or organization should evaluate, and design and/or select these units in accordance with its own functional, environmental, and aesthetic criteria.

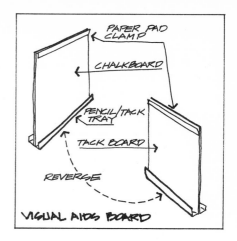

VISUAL AIDS BOARD

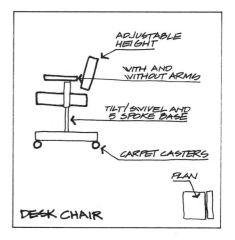

DESK CHAIR

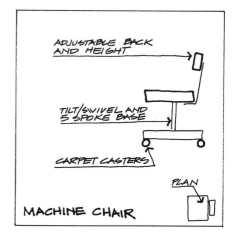

MACHINE CHAIR

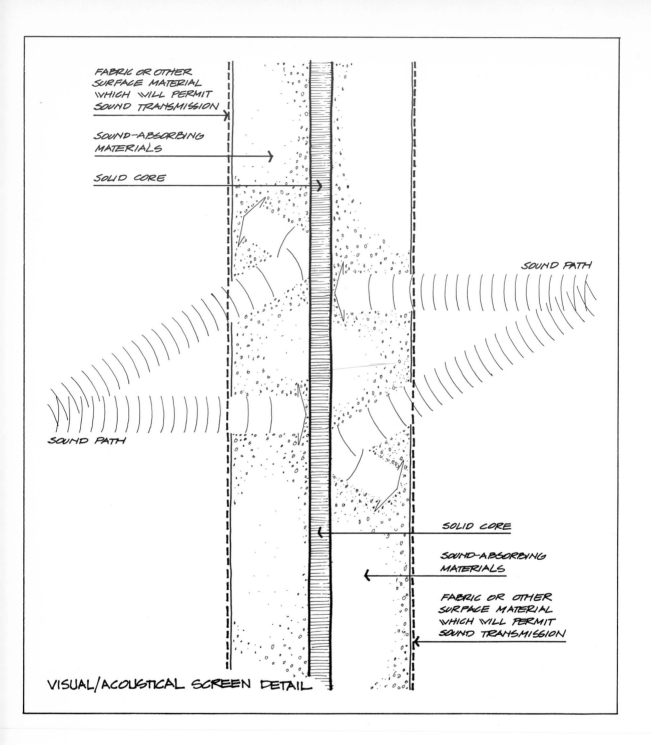

FABRIC OR OTHER
SURFACE MATERIAL
WHICH WILL PERMIT
SOUND TRANSMISSION

SOUND-ABSORBING
MATERIALS

SOLID CORE

SOUND PATH

SOUND PATH

SOLID CORE

SOUND-ABSORBING
MATERIALS

FABRIC OR OTHER
SURFACE MATERIAL
WHICH WILL PERMIT
SOUND TRANSMISSION

VISUAL/ACOUSTICAL SCREEN DETAIL

Screens Screens provide privacy for individual workplaces, as well as for group and conference areas. Since privacy is visual and acoustical separation, these units are correctly called visual/acoustical screens. However, screens also help provide dimension or perspective in the open environment, and they define subjective space, the immediate area with which a person identifies.

Normally, screens are almost flush with the floor, about as wide as a desk is long, and are available in two heights. The higher screen is designed to provide visual privacy for a standing person, and the lower screen for a seated person. In a typical open-landscape area, there are considerably more low screens than high ones; the high ones are usually placed around conference areas.

The surface of the screen is usually fabric, porous enough to permit sound transmission, but thick and strong enough to hold its shape. Although straight screens are manufactured, most office landscape designers strongly recommend that curved screens be used. The curve, in the vertical plane, aids the stability of the unit and discourages users from rearranging the screens into rectangular shapes.

The unit is solid on both sides from top to floor, for visual privacy. Acoustically, however, the construction of the screen is complex. Because the screen usually separates two areas and must absorb sound generated on either side, it must function, acoustically, as two screens. This is accomplished by sandwich construction consisting of, from the face of one side to the face of the other, a surface, a sound-absorbing material, a sound-deadening core, a sound-absorbing material, and the other surface. What happens acoustically is that sounds generated on one side of the screen pass through the surface and are partially absorbed by the sound-absorbing material. The sounds then reach the core and are reflected back into the absorptive material, where whatever remains of the original sound is dissipated. The result of this process is that sound generated on either side of a screen does not penetrate the other side. But sound does not travel in a straight line; rather, it travels in an enlarging cone from the sound source; thus it could travel over, and around, a screen. This does not present a problem because

SIDE CHAIR

PLAN

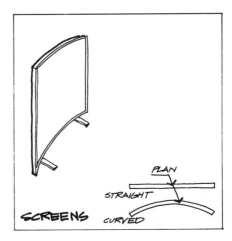

SCREENS

PLAN

STRAIGHT

CURVED

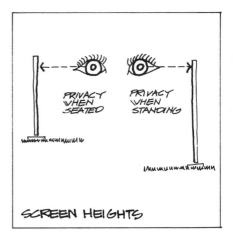

PRIVACY WHEN SEATED

PRIVACY WHEN STANDING

SCREEN HEIGHTS

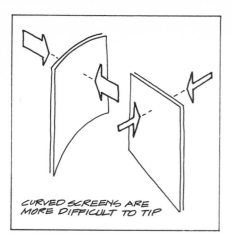

CURVED SCREENS ARE MORE DIFFICULT TO TIP

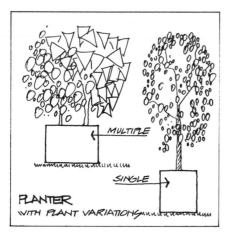

MULTIPLE

SINGLE

PLANTER
WITH PLANT VARIATIONS

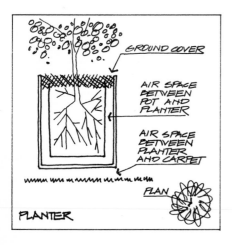

GROUND COVER

AIR SPACE BETWEEN POT AND PLANTER

AIR SPACE BETWEEN PLANTER AND CARPET

PLAN

PLANTER

sounds which pass above the screen are controlled by the ceiling, and sounds that may go around can be controlled by workplace layout.

NOTE: *The design and/or selection of screens is critical to the overall acoustical balance of the open-landscape environment. Many types of screens are produced by many manufacturers. It is essential to use screens with very high sound-absorption coefficients throughout a broad frequency range.*

Safety is a major consideration in screen construction. The selection of the inner-core sound-absorbing material must not only meet the minimum sound-absorption coefficients, but must also be fireproof; that is, it will not burn, support a fire, or give off toxic fumes if subjected to heat or flames. The surface, frame, and core of the unit must also be fireproof. Another safety consideration is tipping. The screen must have feet designed to prevent it from toppling over should someone bump or run into the unit. The feet should also provide adjustment for uneven floors.

Plants and Planters Plants may be used to identify status, ensure adequate distances between workplaces and groups, and define corridors in the open office, but their psychological functions are probably more important. They enhance the environment aesthetically and soften the overall effect of the office on its users and visitors.

Plants should be large, with several plant types in each planter, and each should have its own pot so it can be replaced without interfering with other plants in the planter. Typically, there are four plants per planter, initially forming a regular shape about 3 feet across and the same height as a low screen. As the plants grow, the group should be shaped until it reaches the height of the larger screens, when selected plants should be replaced with smaller new ones.

The department usually negotiates a contract for the purchase and installation of plants and planters based on specifications determined by the planning team with the aid of a plant specialist. But plant maintenance must also be considered, and is generally arranged by contract with a local nursery. An important issue in negotiating the plant maintenance contract is plant replacement. Since the nursery benefits from the office by replacing large plants with smaller ones, it is not uncommon for the nursery to provide weekly plant maintenance, including watering, feeding, pruning, and shaping, in exchange for the large plants it replaces. This arrangement benefits the organization because it requires only an initial cost for the plants.

NOTE: *The growth of plants in an open-plan office is phenomenal. Not only do the constant temperature, humidity, and lighting levels positively affect them, but the activity and proximity of people also seem to quicken their growth.*

Planters should adequately accommodate four large plant pots, including space around the tops of the pots for easy removal, and ample room at the bottom to minimize the possibility of root rot. The planters should be lined and waterproofed, equipped with carpet casters or glides for easy relocation, and should sit close to the floor. The exteriors of the planters may be of any material aesthetically compatible with other furniture and furnishings.

Wardrobe   One of the fundamentals of office landscape planning is that the workplace is for work and work tools, not storage of personal belongings. It is not uncommon to find articles of clothing, personal purchases, and pharmaceutical supplies occupying space designed for work materials. While the user should not be discouraged from having these occasionally needed personal items, he/she should be discouraged from storing them at the workplace. Hence an alternative must be provided, and the wardrobe unit is ideal. This is a storage unit for overcoats, raincoats, hats, overshoes, umbrellas, and personal items of all descriptions. Each unit is usually designed for ten people, including adequate storage for overcoats, etc., and lockable cabinets for other personal belongings.

If the wardrobe units are freestanding—they function very well as screens for lounge areas—the sides and backs should function as visual/acoustical screens, providing sound absorption for the areas adjacent to the units. In some installations, wardrobe units are built into the walls, so that only the usable side is apparent. In either case, the units should be near floor entrances and exits, and toilet and lounge facilities.

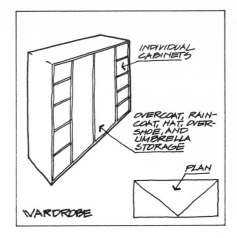

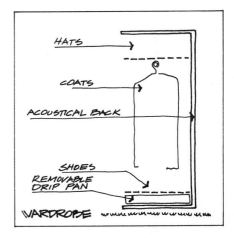

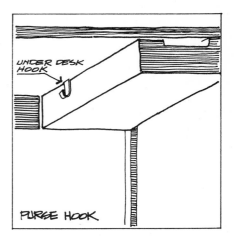

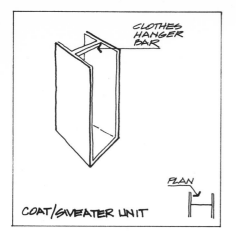

COAT/SWEATER UNIT

COAT TREE

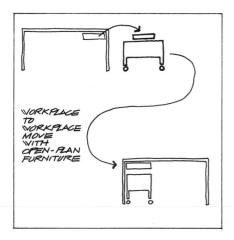

Each unit should be self-ventilating, and the lockable cabinets should be as secure as is economically feasible. A removable drip pan should be provided beneath the coat, shoe, and umbrella storage, and the unit should be as lightweight as possible while meeting the other criteria.

Other Furnishings   It is beyond the scope of this section to enumerate and describe all the special furnishings found in open-landscape areas. Each office landscape project invariably produces items unique to the department being planned for. However, there are two small but common problems which warrant discussion: the storage of purses, jackets, suitcoats, and sweaters.

Some users choose to store purses in wardrobe units; others prefer to have them at their workplaces. A solution which has worked well for workplace storage is to attach a hook beneath the desk. This keeps the purse off the floor and out of the file cart while providing reasonable security when the user is away from his/her workplace.

Wardrobe units may seem an obvious solution to the second problem, but if the user enjoys working without a jacket or suitcoat, she/he may find it inconvenient to retrieve her/his jacket or suitcoat from the wardrobe each time a visitor arrives or a meeting must be attended. In some installations, special coat units have been designed to serve small groups of people. However, conventional coat-trees seem to function just as well, provided they are aesthetically compatible with other furnishings. In either case, jacket and suitcoat storage at the workplace should be considered; otherwise screens and visual aids boards are used, and hanging coats on screens compromises their intended functions.

CONVENTIONAL FURNITURE

At some point in almost every open-landscape project, a question is raised concerning the continued use of the department's existing conventional furniture. Of course the furniture can be used, but if it does not meet the criteria for open-plan furniture, it will cause functional and psychological handicaps.

One example of a functional handicap involves the workplace desk and individual file cart. With open-landscape furniture, exchanging individual workplaces is a simple matter of removing the desk utility drawers, placing them on top of the file carts, and rolling them to the new workplaces where the drawers are slipped into the existing desks. This can be accomplished in a matter of minutes without special tools or the aid of maintenance personnel. The same exchange, using conventional furniture, requires either moving the desks or emptying the drawers and file pedestals, and transporting the contents by box to the new workplaces. Consequently, many moves involving conventional furniture are never considered. In short, conventional furniture handicaps open-landscape flexibility.

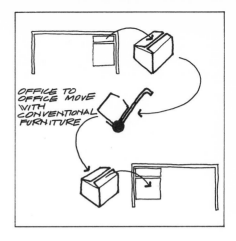

OFFICE TO OFFICE MOVE WITH CONVENTIONAL FURNITURE

Psychologically, the consequences may be greater, or are at least more constant. As mentioned earlier in this section, conventional furniture in an open landscape creates a feeling of being closed in. And though additional space may be provided, when extra utility requirements and communication and work-flow slowdowns are considered, this generally proves to be more costly than supplying the proper furniture.

The aesthetic environment is also very important psychologically. While individuals can be permitted to furnish their own conventional office spaces with the *damnedest things,* it is another story when many individuals are asked to accept and live with these oddments in an open area.

KEEPING EXISTING CONVENTIONAL FURNITURE FOR A NEW OPEN-PLAN OFFICE

COMPROMISES

EFFICIENCY
FLEXIBILITY
AESTHETICS

The point is that the department should consider all the consequences carefully before choosing to use its existing and/or conventional furniture in the open landscape. Unfortunately, existing furniture is not taken in trade, and used furniture has little market value. However, the compromises in efficiency, flexibility, and aesthetics may, in the long run, cost more than selecting furniture and furnishings which meet the criteria established for the project.

NOTE: *The specific furniture and furnishings criteria /rationales below are included to summarize and supplement those mentioned in this section. However, it is important to note that these criteria /rationales can and should be expanded and varied in an actual project.*

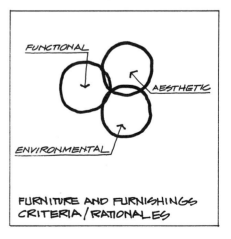

FUNCTIONAL

AESTHETIC

ENVIRONMENTAL

FURNITURE AND FURNISHINGS CRITERIA / RATIONALES

Functional Considerations

- *Furniture should be of standardized design—to minimize investment costs and simplify inventory.*
- *Workplace requirements should be met by a combination of standard components—to minimize furniture variety and allow maximum flexibility.*
- *Furniture should be rigidly constructed—to avoid vibration and assure stability.*
- *Furniture should be lightweight—to aid workplace flexibility.*
- *Furniture should be designed for maximum comfort—to promote efficiency and well-being.*
- *Components should be easily moved without special tools or equipment—to facilitate rapid rearrangement and replacement at minimum cost.*
- *Furniture design should have adequate floor clearance—to allow easy cleaning.*
- *Frequently used files should not be enclosed—to minimize search/access time and aid in maintaining orderly files.*
- *Workplace filing equipment should be mobile and separate from the desk—to minimize the furniture moved in workplace rearrangement and to allow files to be moved to any place of need.*
- *Workplace file carts should be designed for a seated person and contain files at one level only—to allow easy access.*
- *Group files should be at two levels—to conserve space.*
- *Workplace and group file carts should contain suspended files which accommodate the most frequently used paper sizes: letter, legal, and computer printouts—to provide maximum flexibility for materials storage and to allow the user to remove materials easily.*
- *File carts should be accessible from the top—to provide quick, easy filing and retrieval with maximum visibility of material.*
- *Central/archive files should be contained in open shelves extending from floor to approximately 6 feet above floor—to conserve space and maintain convenience and safety.*
- *Bound materials at the workplace should be on*

open bookshelves which are usable from both sides—to conserve space and bookcase costs and permit usage by more than one person.

- Workplace and group file carts should be modular units—to provide flexibility and allow expansion.

- Furniture and equipment casters and glides should be oversized—to permit easy use on carpets.

- Furniture edges should be smooth and round—to prevent injury to persons and clothing.

- Visual aids boards and visual/acoustical screens should be equipped with long, but thin and narrow, feet—to prevent the units from tipping, and to prevent individuals from tripping over the feet.

Environmental Considerations

- Work surfaces should be nonreflecting with low color/tone contrasts between surfaces and work papers—to reduce eye strain.

- Furniture and equipment should have minimum vertical sound-reflective surfaces—to aid, not hinder, the overall acoustical balance of the space.

- Furniture should be open, transparent, with as few skirts and panels as feasible—to prevent the user from feeling crowded or closed in and to allow more complete sound control.

- Drawers, doors, casters, and other potential noise producers should be designed for quiet operation—to eliminate disturbing and unexpected noises.

Aesthetic Considerations

- Furniture should enhance the office environment—to affect office work positively and to attract potential employees.

- Pieces of furniture designed and/or selected should be compatible with the overall open landscape—to provide an aesthetically pleasing environment.

- Lounge furniture should be different from workplace furniture—to provide psychological as well as physical breaks from office work.

- Heights of furniture types (screens, plants, visual aids boards, bookcases) should vary—to eliminate a potential visual plane between floor and ceiling.

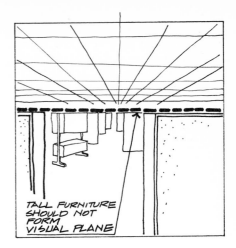

TALL FURNITURE SHOULD NOT FORM VISUAL PLANE

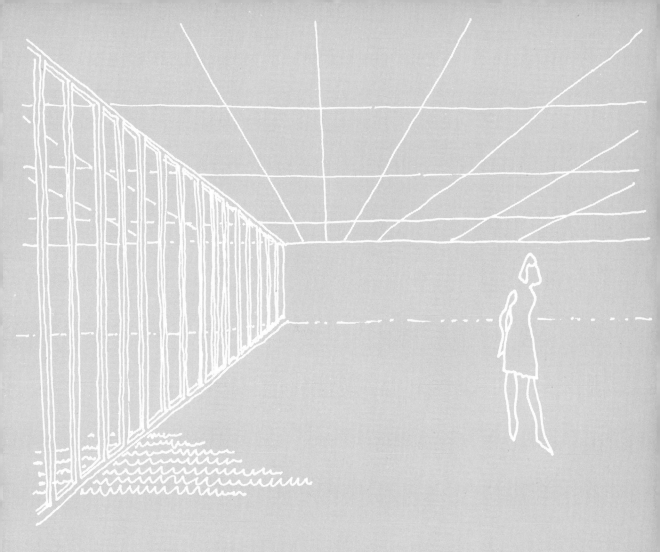

Section Five

The
Facility

B ecause movable items, those contained within the facility such as furniture and furnishings, are discussed elsewhere in the book, this section will be limited to the fixed elements of the building.

SPACE CONFIGURATION

The building's shape and square footage per floor is invariably affected by site limitations and building codes if the facility is new, and existing constraints if it is leased or renovated. However, the correlation diagram discussed in Section Three establishes the ideal locations of departmental tally groups as determined by communication and work flow, and with the addition of workplace calculations also determines the total square footage required for the department and the ideal separation, by floor, of its groups. The importance of following the correlation diagram in designing the facility cannot be overstated, and though compromises are inevitable, they should be held to a minimum.

A large square or rectangular space is ideal for an effective, functional open landscape. This proportion permits many departmental elements to exist in close proximity on a single floor, allowing maximum accessibility for interaction. If the department's tally groups are scattered vertically, interaction becomes more difficult and efficiency is impaired. A large, square space also facilitates group rearrangement if interaction patterns are altered. Further, this space configuration increases the ratio of interior space to exterior wall surface, desirable because interior space is less expensive to construct—square foot for square foot—than exterior walls.

Shapes other than squares and rectangles, such as circles, polygons, and trapezoids, form fat spaces and can create pleasant work areas, but they are usually more expensive to construct. The additional costs come from using standard rectangular building materials to construct nonrectangular shapes. Even the costs of monolithic building materials, such as concrete, increase because the formwork is manufactured in rectangles. This problem does not stop with the exterior of the building; such things as ceiling and flooring materials are also conventionally rectangular. This is

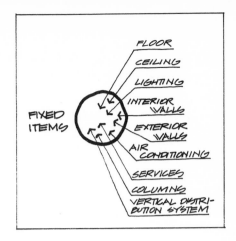

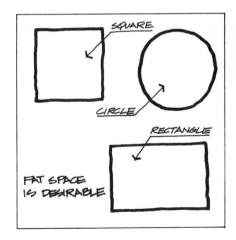

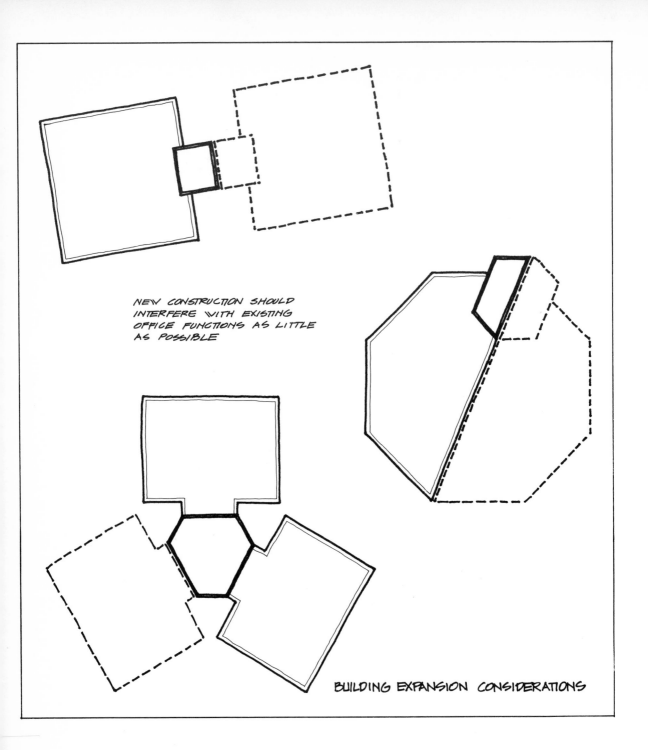

NEW CONSTRUCTION SHOULD
INTERFERE WITH EXISTING
OFFICE FUNCTIONS AS LITTLE
AS POSSIBLE

BUILDING EXPANSION CONSIDERATIONS

certainly not to discourage experimentation or innovation in office building design, but simply to point out that, unfortunately, premium costs may be incurred when building design deviates from the norm.

Another consideration in building space configuration is expansion. Just as they function horizontally, demonstrated by the chart of hierarchy and function, departments expand horizontally, and expansion space should imitate the department's projected growth. However, this is easier said than done. Obviously the building site is a controlling factor. If the building is sited in a downtown metropolitan area, land cost or lack of availability could prohibit horizontal expansion, whereas a suburban or rural site would probably permit it. In either case, if the department is growing, building design must allow for expansion.

Facilities such as central air conditioning and fixed areas like kitchen and dining, recreation, parking, storage, archives, etc., should be easily accessible to employees without causing functional difficulties for departmental or organizational expansion. Ideally, these facilities should be collected at the bottom or top of the building. The lower portions of the building are especially recommended for areas where large numbers of people gather, such as auditoriums or cafeterias, in order to provide adequate emergency exits, though local building codes often dictate the placement of these areas.

Just as a building floor can be too small to meet the communication and work-flow needs of an organization, it can also be too large. At some point, getting from one end of a floor to the other requires more time than getting to another floor by stairs or elevator. Because there is no norm for this breaking point, it must be determined for the given project by the planning team.

NOTE: *There is an ongoing debate among office landscape planners over minimum and maximum sizes for open-landscape areas. This debate will probably never be resolved because of the variations between project needs and sizes. However, there does seem to be an accepted common denominator for determining minimum areas: acoustical balance.*

The minimum number of workplaces in a given area is usually determined by the background noise

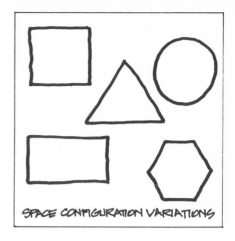

SPACE CONFIGURATION VARIATIONS

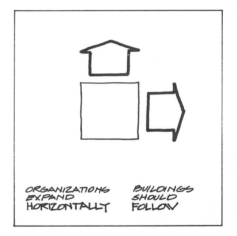

ORGANIZATIONS EXPAND HORIZONTALLY   BUILDINGS SHOULD FOLLOW

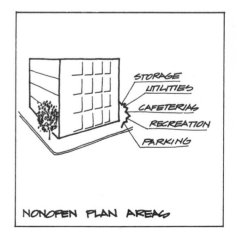

STORAGE
UTILITIES
CAFETERIAS
RECREATION
PARKING

NONOPEN PLAN AREAS

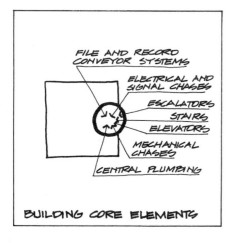

ACOUSTICS USUALLY DETERMINE
MINIMUM SIZE OPEN PLANS

MAXIMUM SIZE OPEN PLANS
ARE USUALLY GOVERNED BY
BUILDING CODES AND/OR
DISTANCE BETWEEN
ORGANIZATIONAL SUBUNITS

FILE AND RECORD
CONVEYOR SYSTEMS
ELECTRICAL AND
SIGNAL CHASES
ESCALATORS
STAIRS
ELEVATORS
MECHANICAL
CHASES
CENTRAL PLUMBING

BUILDING CORE ELEMENTS

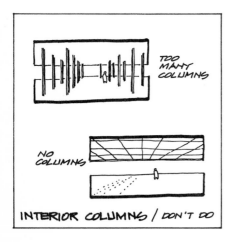

TOO
MANY
COLUMNS

NO
COLUMNS

INTERIOR COLUMNS / DON'T DO

level created by the people and machines in the space. If this level drops too low, the acoustical balance is upset and privacy is impaired. Because planned-for departments vary greatly in types of tasks performed and numbers of workplaces left empty for varying lengths of time, an acoustical consultant is necessary as a specialist on the planning team in order to calculate the minimum number of workplaces required for acoustical balance.

It should also be mentioned, though, that a background sound system may be installed to increase a below-standard or erratic background noise level. This system will be discussed in detail later in this section.

The maximum number of workplaces in a given area is often governed by building codes. Some codes require that square footage above a certain figure must be divided by fire walls and/or sprinklered. If this is the case, and if all other considerations are equal, it is usually more economical to design more floors than oversized ones separated by fire walls.

If there is a rule of thumb for viable extremes of floor sizes, it is 100 ± workplaces as a minimum and 500 ± as a maximum. Immediately, though, it must be added that smaller and larger open office landscapes have been installed which function, and function well.

Vertical transportation elements should also be considered in the building's space configuration. These include stairs, elevators, escalators, file and record conveyor systems, electrical and signal closets, mechanical chases, and central plumbing. It is advantageous to collect rather than separate these vertical elements, from the point of view of both building-construction economy and departmental work-flow efficiency.

The most common reference point for all users is the entry/exit, and for this reason, shared facilities involving vertical elements should be collected here. This means the floor service center is logically located at the vertical conveyor system, the floor reception area at the entry/exit, employee lounges near toilet facilities, and enclosed conference areas near the entry/exit for the convenience of business associates and personnel located on other floors. If these more or less fixed areas and the vertical transportation elements are collected, the rest of the floor is left free for rearranging workplaces as changing tasks dictate, and optimum interior flexibility and conditions for group interaction are achieved.

Structurally, the interior space must be supported, and though it is possible to eliminate interior columns in some building-design configurations, this is often psychologically undesirable. In a columnless space, especially a large one, there are few spatial reference points and the open landscape tends to vanish into the exterior walls. Interior columns help provide dimension and perspective, and define the subjective areas with which individuals and groups identify. The columns must be spaced so that they do not hamper workplace layout, and should be at least 30 feet apart.

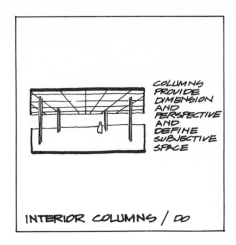

INTERIOR COLUMNS / DO

BUILDING SHELL

The building shell is defined here as the fixed items of the facility, including floor, ceiling, interior and exterior walls, power and signal distribution, and background sound system.

Floor The floor is one of the two largest planes within the facility—the other is the ceiling—and plays a major role in acoustics, making carpeting a necessity. The acoustical requirements of the carpet are determined by the overall acoustical qualities of the given space: its ceiling type, furniture, and number and types of visual/acoustical screens. Basically, the carpet should absorb a spectrum of sound frequencies directed toward or reflected into it. Since the carpet will probably be made of synthetic fibers with no sound-absorptive qualities, it should be backed with a sound-absorptive material so that sound passing through the carpet fibers is absorbed by the backing. Sound not absorbed by the backing on entering the carpet is reflected by the floor and absorbed on its way out. The carpet backing, then, works the same way as the sound-absorbing material in a visual/acoustical screen.

Other important considerations are carpet color and utility. For instance, the carpet should not show dirt easily, no imprints should remain when furniture is rearranged, and it should either not produce static electricity or have static electricity reduction qualities. It should also be dense enough for carpet casters, al-

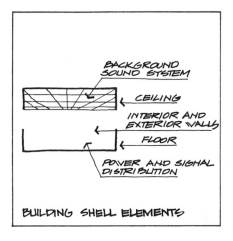

BUILDING SHELL ELEMENTS

FLOOR

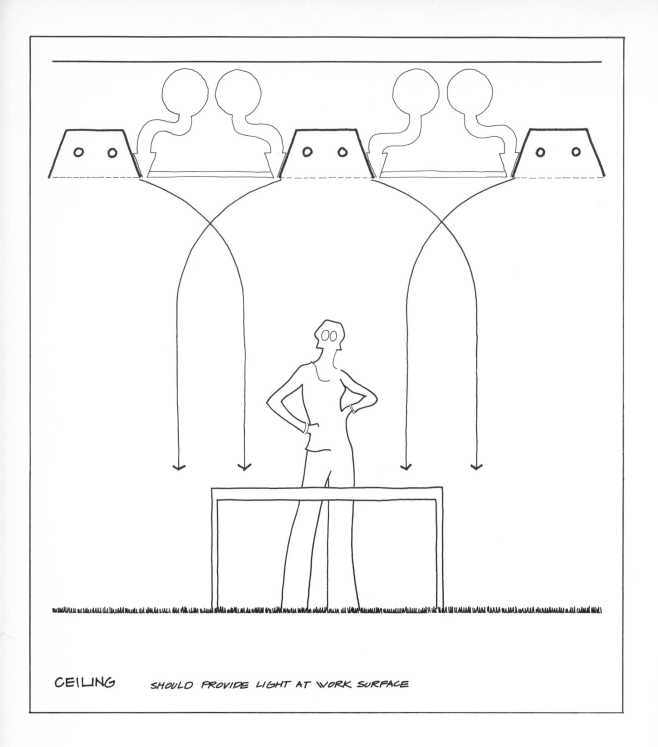

CEILING   SHOULD PROVIDE LIGHT AT WORK SURFACE

CEILING   AIR SHOULD MOVE VERTICALLY

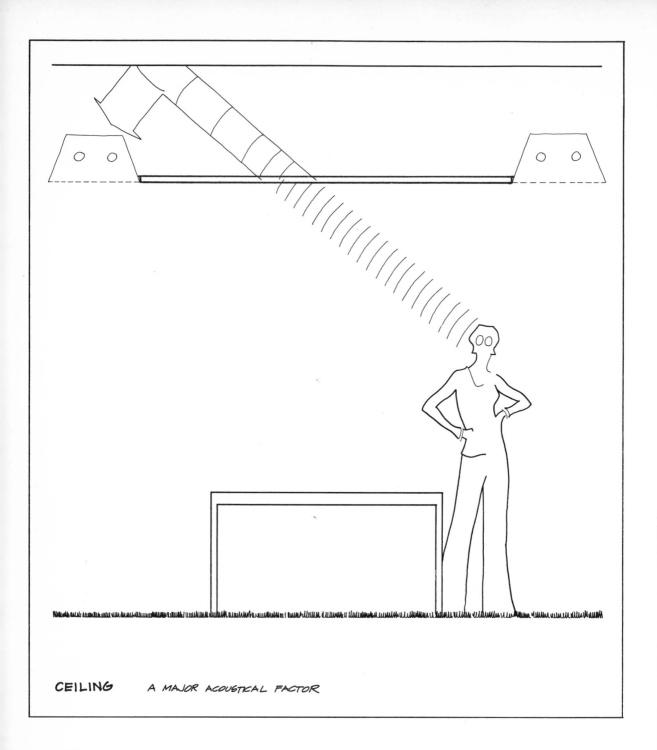

CEILING   A MAJOR ACOUSTICAL FACTOR

lowing chair movement without the use of floor pads. If the electrical and signal systems are brought through the floor, the edges of the carpet should not ravel, and when electrical service is moved, carpet plugs should not be visible.

The carpet should also be selected for its firesafety characteristics. Most carpets meet firesafety standards for combustion, especially when adhered to the structural floor, but when raised to certain temperatures, some backing materials give off toxic fumes at least as dangerous as flames.

Carpets without patterns function best in open areas. If a patterned carpet is desired, the pattern should be small and nondirectional so that it does not interfere with workplace orientation or rearrangement.

Ceiling The most obvious functional requirement for the ceiling in an open-landscape environment is that it house the lighting supply. Lighting must be adequate at the work-surface level and should be evenly distributed throughout the space to allow maximum workplace flexibility and rearrangement.

The ceiling is the largest uninterrupted plane in the facility and is therefore the most important single acoustical element. Like the carpet, the acoustical qualities of the ceiling should be balanced with other elements in the landscape. The ceiling material absorbs sound the same way visual/acoustical screens and carpets do: sound passes through the finished ceiling material, where some of it is absorbed, then reflects off the structural ceiling and back into the material. The entire ceiling, however, cannot be sound-absorptive because of light fixtures and air diffusers. If additional sound absorption is needed, vertical baffles may be installed below and/or above the finished ceiling, or it may be coffered. Baffling or coffering makes it possible for all sounds reaching the ceiling to be completely absorbed.

Coffered, flat with baffles below, eggcrate with baffles above, and flat ceilings can be used successfully. All these variations can contain lighting and air-distribution systems, as well as sound-absorbing materials. Although it is possible to install a flat ceiling that is acoustically sufficient, it may be better psychologically to break the plane and interrupt the vastness of the

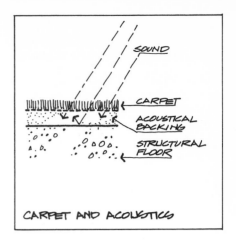

CARPET AND ACOUSTICS

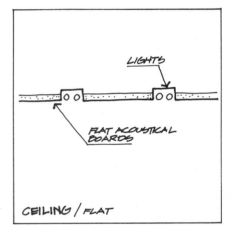

CEILING / FLAT

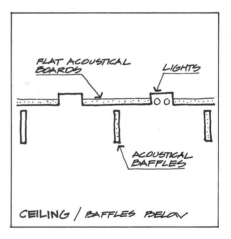

CEILING / BAFFLES BELOW

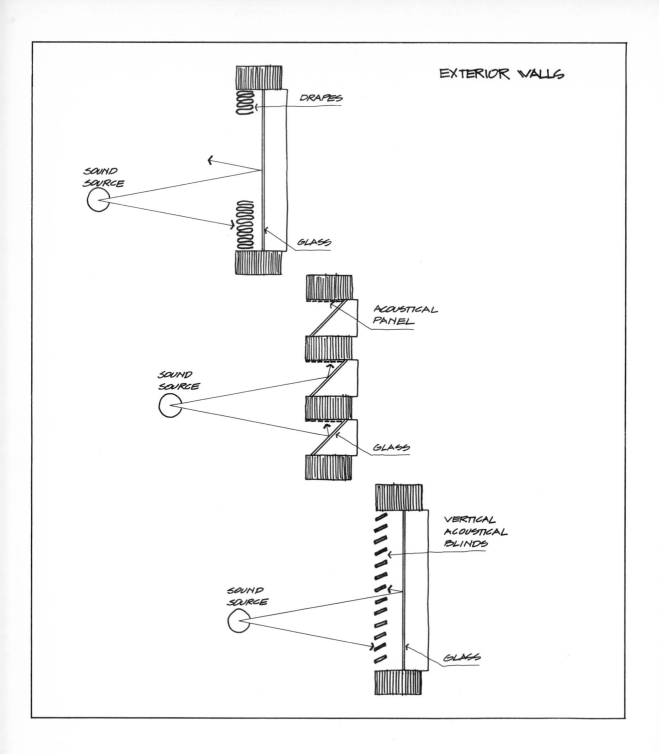

EXTERIOR WALLS

DRAPES

SOUND SOURCE

GLASS

ACOUSTICAL PANEL

SOUND SOURCE

GLASS

VERTICAL ACOUSTICAL BLINDS

SOUND SOURCE

GLASS

ceiling. This helps the user define distance, and individual and group spaces.

Both heating and cooling air should be supplied and returned vertically through the ceiling, and air movement should be distributed over an area large enough that it is not detectable. A horizontal air-flow system invariably creates uncomfortable, unhealthy drafts, and should be avoided.

It is important to design air and lighting supplies that do not need to be altered with workplace rearrangements. In addition, totally uniform systems are lower in cost than movable ones, both initially and over an extended period.

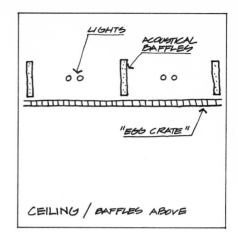

CEILING / BAFFLES ABOVE

Interior Walls If electrical and communication equipment, or conference and special areas make it necessary to install interior walls which protrude into the space, these walls should absorb rather than reflect sound. This is easily accomplished by covering the walls with carpeting or other sound-absorbing material such as flat panels which function like visual/acoustical screens. Unless interior columns are exceptionally large, as they sometimes are in older buildings, they usually do not have to be sound-absorbing.

Exterior Walls Exterior walls generally include windows, which create acoustical problems because glass is a highly sound-reflective material. One solution is to use acoustical drapes, but this is unsatisfactory. If the drapes are closed, the purpose of the windows is defeated because one cannot see outside; and if the drapes are opened, the glass is left to reflect noise generated within the space.

A more successful solution to the problem is to design windows in which the glass sits at an angle and reflects sound into sound-absorbing panels. The drawback here is that the thickness of the exterior wall is increased, adding considerably to the cost of the facility. However, if this approach is economically feasible, the method is an effective and desirable one.

A third solution, both acoustically and economically sound, is the use of vertical/acoustical blinds. In any position, these blinds have sound-absorbing qualities and, of course, when opened, permit looking through

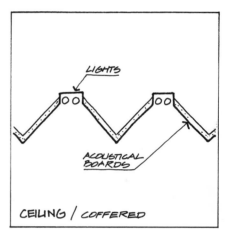

CEILING / COFFERED

INTERIOR WALLS SHOULD ABSORB RATHER THAN REFLECT SOUND

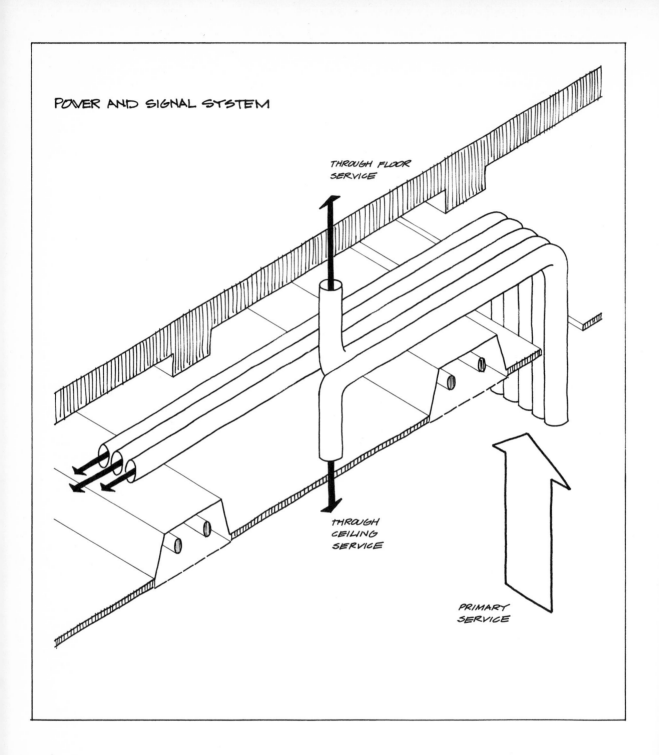

POWER AND SIGNAL SYSTEM

THROUGH FLOOR
SERVICE

THROUGH
CEILING
SERVICE

PRIMARY
SERVICE

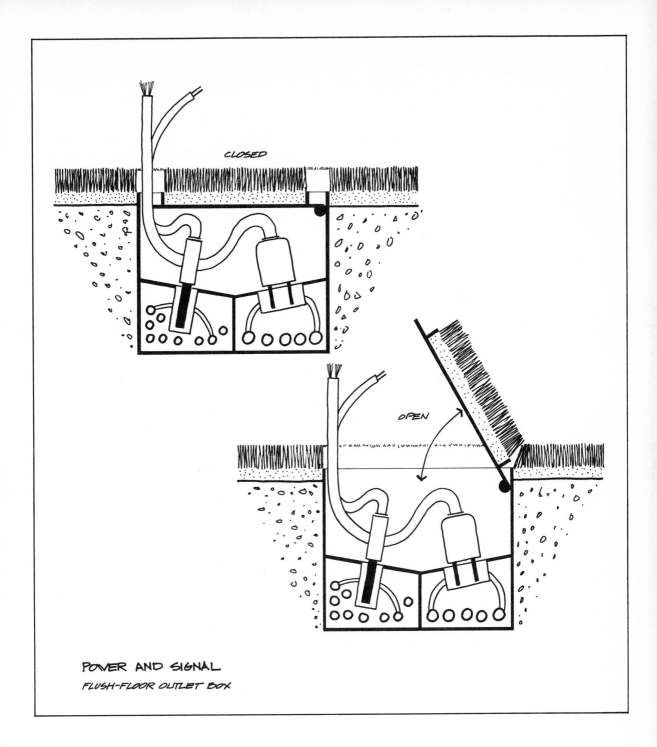

CLOSED

OPEN

POWER AND SIGNAL
FLUSH-FLOOR OUTLET BOX

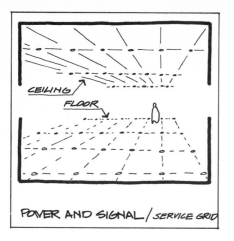

POWER AND SIGNAL / SERVICE GRID

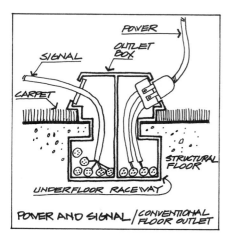

POWER AND SIGNAL / CONVENTIONAL FLOOR OUTLET

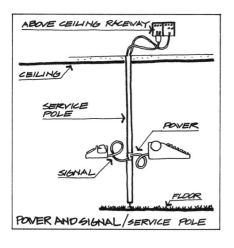

POWER AND SIGNAL / SERVICE POLE

the windows. With increasing popularity, vertical blinds are becoming more economical. They are easily maintained and, when installed in typical 5- or 6-foot sections, vary the otherwise regular patterns of the walls.

Power and Signal   Power and signal pertains to telephone, electrical, computer, intracommunications systems, and other wiring required in the facility. The need is to convey the wiring to the work surface, and whether this is accomplished by bringing it through the floor or the ceiling, the basic distributive system is the same. Major service is supplied vertically through the building at the service core. At each floor, feeder lines spread horizontally in patterns which permit power and signal service throughout the space. If the feeders are in the ceiling, they are usually in the plenum, the space between the finished and structural ceilings; if in the floor, they can either be in the ceiling plenum of the floor below, or in conduits within the structural floor topping. In all three cases, the feeder-distribution system is, for all practical purposes, the same.

Outlet boxes which sit on the carpet are conventionally used if the wiring is brought through the floor. These are connected to the feeder-distribution system through holes in the carpet, so each time workplaces are rearranged and some of the outlet boxes must be replaced, new holes must be cut and the existing ones plugged. This is a time-consuming process and increases the cost of workplace rearrangement.

A more viable solution for floor power and signal is outlet boxes flush with the carpet. These are installed in a grid pattern which permits service to any workplace arrangement. When new service is needed, a small lid, flush with the floor, is opened, the equipment requiring service is plugged into the box, and the lid is closed. Removing workplace service is equally simple. This system of flush, fixed outlet boxes is quick, easy, and virtually maintenance-free. Although the cost of installing these outlets is somewhat higher than that of installing the above-floor outlets, the difference is quickly made up by the maintenance saved.

NOTE: *In Europe, flush-floor outlet boxes are the rule rather than the exception. They have been used in numerous installations in the United States and Canada, but are not permitted by some local building codes.*

If service is brought to the work surfaces through the ceiling, the wiring can be contained in vertical service poles. These poles are easily rearranged if the ceiling is designed with a grid system to accommodate them. The grid can be constructed of runners which permit pole plug-in at any point, or it can contain hidden outlets for plug-in at predetermined places. Service poles are usually unnoticeable in the open space and do not detract from it aesthetically. Further, it is possible to diminish the number of service poles needed by using outlets in columns and exterior walls. An additional advantage of this solution is that containing the wiring within the ceiling plenum is usually less costly than an under-floor duct system. This is especially true in renovations where under-floor duct systems do not already exist.

Background Sound System   In any open plan, people and machines create background noise, but if this noise level is irregular or unpredictable, the result is frequent acoustical imbalance. For this reason, acousticians often choose to supplement background noise with a specially designed and controlled system of sound. Sometimes called *pink noise* or *white sound,* this system produces a soft, continuous, pervasive sound in the frequency range and volume needed for the acoustical balance of the space.

The sound is usually generated from boxes hung in a pattern of overlapping grids in the ceiling plenum, with the control unit for each floor located at the service core area. It is important for the system to be designed so that the sound sources cannot be discerned. If they are detectable, the system will probably distract the users. In successful installations, most users forget the system is even there.

In some installations, single sound-frequency systems have been used; however, more sophisticated multiple-frequency units have been developed which are less discernable than their predecessors. But whichever system is used, the acoustical specialist must tune it for the space it serves. Once the system is correctly tuned, it seldom needs further adjustment.

The primary reason for acoustically balancing the open landscape is to provide its users with single-room

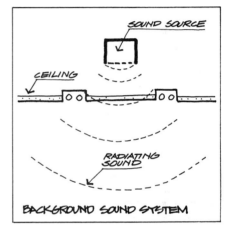

BACKGROUND SOUND SYSTEM

BACKGROUND SOUND SYSTEM

privacy. Because this cannot be achieved at the last minute, it is essential for the acoustical consultant to be involved in all elements of environmental planning.

NOTE: *Invariably, the question of using background music is raised at some point in the project. Not only do most acousticians strongly discourage background music because of its frequency and volume variations, but most office users find it distracting, especially over a long period of time.*

SECURITY

In most offices, personal belongings are a major security concern. But if security for these items is planned for, and the recommendations in Section Four for purses, jackets, etc., are followed, then probably few cases of theft will occur. In addition, the open landscape has an advantage over the conventional office in that workplaces are more visible and their contents are therefore less susceptible to theft.

Occasionally, the main tasks of certain groups or departments are directly related to classified records and materials. In these instances, lockable file units generally provide adequate security. Tighter security is needed for groups or departments working with cash or related items. Two of the more successful ways this has been handled are providing a vault where money and related records can be stored, and separating the group by a security screen which does not interfere with the space acoustically or aesthetically.

Overall floor security must be provided, though this is probably a greater concern where several different organizations are housed in the same facility than where one organization occupies a whole building. In either situation, floor receptionists give adequate security during normal working hours. For off-hours, the most common security measure is to lock staircase doors, and use floor-keyed elevators. It is also possible to separate the elevator and stair lobby from the open landscape by lockable doors or gates. However, this solution does not function well unless the doors can be folded out of the way during normal working hours.

NOTE: *The following list of facility criteria is included to supplement the sample criteria cited in this section:*

SECURITY SCREEN

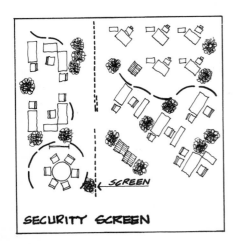

SCREEN

SECURITY SCREEN

- In general, the facility should allow work-flow and communication processes to function optimally.
- The building should facilitate workplace rearrangement without structural alterations.
- As much as possible, the facility should accommodate the group and workplace arrangements established by the correlation diagram.
- Groups which have a great deal of communication with each other should not be separated vertically.
- Office areas should be divided by as few permanent walls as possible.
- Columns should not divide the office area or hinder rearrangement of workplaces. Generally, there should be no less than 30 feet between columns.
- Every part of the open landscape should enjoy the same conditions of lighting, air conditioning, and acoustics.
- A 5-foot grid usually works well for telephone and electricity outlet systems.
- The floor should have a load-bearing capacity which allows installation of all necessary furniture and equipment in any location in the office.
- It should be possible to look out of the windows from any workplace.
- The optically effective height of the open area should be about 9 feet. Greater height gives less acoustical privacy.
- The lighting of the office area should provide equally pleasant working conditions for all workplaces. Generally, light intensity should be 100 footcandles after 50 percent of normal usage.
- The temperature and humidity of the office should be fully controlled.
- The acoustical balance of the office should guarantee that normal conversations cannot be understood beyond 18 feet, or 12 feet with screens.
- Fire detection and alarm systems should be installed in the facility. Sprinkler systems should be installed in storage areas.
- Facility configuration and siting should allow horizontal expansion without disturbing work in the existing open landscape.
- The periphery of the building should be kept as small as possible in relation to interior space.

OPTICALLY EFFECTIVE CEILING HEIGHT IS APPROXIMATELY 9 FEET

NORMAL CONVERSATIONS SHOULD NOT CARRY BEYOND 18 FEET OR BEYOND 12 FEET WITH SCREENS

BUILDING PERIPHERY SHOULD BE AS SMALL AS POSSIBLE IN RELATION TO INTERIOR SPACE

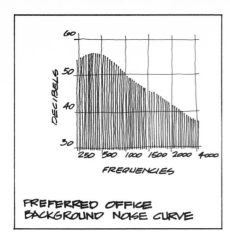

PREFERRED OFFICE
BACKGROUND NOISE CURVE

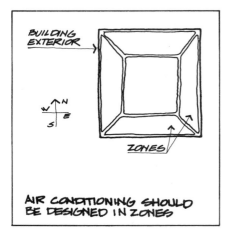

AIR CONDITIONING SHOULD
BE DESIGNED IN ZONES

■ The number of floors should be kept to a minimum, producing large squarish floor areas.

■ All office areas within one floor should be functionally accessible from one point. The entire flow of visitors, personnel, material, and paper from one floor to another should pass through this point of accessibility.

■ Vertical transportation elements should be collected, forming the building core.

■ Special areas related to or requiring vertical transportation elements should be collected at the building core.

■ In order to maximize open-landscape flexibility, the building core should be located to one side of the building.

■ The sound level in the office should be between 50 and 55 decibels (NC 40 to 45) with as little fluctuation as possible.

■ The air-conditioning system should be designed in interior and exterior zones to ensure balanced temperature control at the center and edges of the space.

■ Air speed at the work surface should not exceed 6 inches per second.

■ The rate of fresh air exchange should accommodate the relatively large concentration of office personnel in the open-landscape area.

■ Relative humidity within the office should be between 45 and 55 percent.

■ The noise level generated by the air-conditioning system should be considered in the overall acoustical balance of the space.

■ The entire lighting system should be glare-free. This means the angle of vision to the light source should be no greater than 45 degrees, or light-source shields should be provided.

Section Six

Status
in the
Landscape

People working in office landscapes are rationally aware of the advantages of the open environment: its flexibility and optimization of user interactions. But because many traditional status symbols, such as anterooms, suites, doors, and wall plaques, are not part of the open office landscape, the users must redefine their organizational identities, and some find this initially difficult. Executives and especially middle-management personnel are more comfortable when their statuses within the pecking order of the group are clearly identified and easily recognized by other employees, as well as visitors. Identification of status is critical to the overall acceptance of an open landscape by those working within it, and therefore planners must provide new kinds of visible status and identification symbols that are integrated with the landscape.

User identity and status must be understood, analyzed, and evaluated as they relate negatively and positively to communication and work-flow functions, flexibility, and innovation.

DESCRIPTION

Basically, there seem to be two kinds of status: material and social. *Material status* is essentially having something someone else does not, such as a large office with windows and a certain type or quantity of furniture, a private toilet or key to one, a private parking space, a certain number of secretaries or assistants, or a certain salary. All of these in some way identify a particular level of importance or authority within the organization.

Social status is more difficult to pinpoint, but more often than not it is marked by the freedom to do something to or in the presence of someone who is not allowed to reciprocate. For example: a subordinate must knock before entering a superior's office; a subordinate must be invited to be seated by a superior; a superior remains behind her/his desk in a position of authority while a subordinate sits in a visitor's chair; a subordinate cannot touch or rest on a superior's desk; a superior may put his/her arm around a subordinate, but not vice versa; a superior may joke with or even tease a subordinate, but not vice versa. Further,

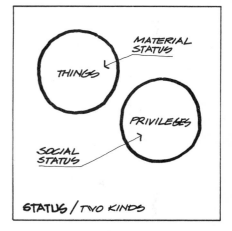

STATUS / TWO KINDS

REVERSE STATUS
CAN BE MATERIAL OR SOCIAL

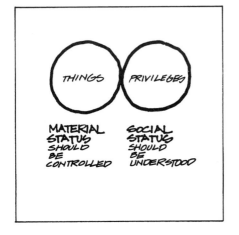

CHANGES
IN
STATUS
DISTRIBUTION
MUST BE
PLANNED
WITH
CHANGES
IN
ORGANIZATIONAL
STRUCTURES

THINGS   PRIVILEGES

MATERIAL   SOCIAL
STATUS   STATUS
SHOULD   SHOULD
BE   BE
CONTROLLED   UNDERSTOOD

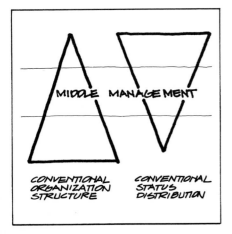

MIDDLE MANAGEMENT

CONVENTIONAL   CONVENTIONAL
ORGANIZATION   STATUS
STRUCTURE   DISTRIBUTION

social status is often gained by seniority and level of education.

Status can also be marked by a reversal of its traditional symbols, whether material or social. This usually involves persons at or near the top of the organization's hierarchy, and manifests itself as an outward shucking of status, but these people are generally so well established that, in fact, no such thing takes place. Examples of reverse status might be giving up a corner office and relocating in a central position, wearing very informal unconventional clothes to work, or taking on tasks normally performed by subordinates. These expressions of a new kind of status are often quickly mimicked by others in the organization.

Status and status symbols are so important to the organizational identities of employees and the definition of their relationships and interactions that any change in organizational structure must include planned changes in status distribution, or confusion and dissatisfaction will result. In large organizations, people tend to lose a sense of their own individuality and seem to try to replace it with status symbols. Often, positions with little status are renamed to give their holders a feeling of more authority than their job functions actually carry. In this way, janitor becomes maintenance superintendent, mail clerk becomes postal manager, and secretary becomes administrative assistant.

The most desirable of all alternatives is, perhaps, to equalize and thereby eliminate status. This is, of course, a matter of opinion and to what degree it is even possible is an open question; and it must be admitted that the chances of making the attempt to equalize material status alone seem minimal. However, if material status may not be discarded, it can be controlled, and personnel at all levels can at least be made aware of the manifestations of social status.

Innovation In many organizations, material status snowballs as employees rise through the hierarchical structure. The more status is amassed, the easier it is to get and the more it is related to seniority and job titles rather than performance. This often arbitrary distribution allows status to become an end in itself and negatively affects the willingness of employees, especially middle management, to develop and/or accept innovation.

Developing and/or endorsing innovation entails a certain amount of risk. Because of their extremes of status, personnel very high or very low in the organization stand to lose smaller or gain larger percentages of status, respectively, than those in the middle. For middle management, what can be lost is about equal to what can be gained, and so innovation is rarely accepted by or generated within this group. The result is that, though lower-level employees have some incentive to innovate, their ideas are usually rejected by midlevel personnel, and innovation is left to the relatively small number of people at the top. Consequently, if middle-management personnel are considered the key to organizational productivity and efficiency, it is necessary to provide them with more status gain for successful innovations than status loss for unsuccessful ones.

It is also necessary to provide effective leadership at all personnel levels. As far as status is concerned, this means rewarding employees for performance, not seniority or job classifications. A leader must have enough imagination, freedom, and security to break from the norm and develop, test, and/or accept innovations. These qualities can be legitimized and supported by reasonably proportioned, systematically distributed status.

Communication In traditional communication patterns, employees at all levels are much freer to transmit information and opinions to their subordinates than vice versa, and the subordinates are encouraged not to offer constructive criticism, but to react passively. This one-way communication flow is strengthened by awarding status for supportive reports made to superiors, which, in turn, often causes subordinates to withhold negative information. The more intensely subordinates desire advancement, then, the less accurately they pass job-related communication on to their superiors. This is less than ideal.

If the planned-for department or organization defines communication basically as report and command, traditional communication patterns must be altered in order to allow full rather than partial reporting.

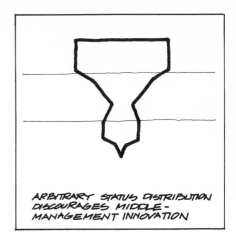

ARBITRARY STATUS DISTRIBUTION DISCOURAGES MIDDLE-MANAGEMENT INNOVATION

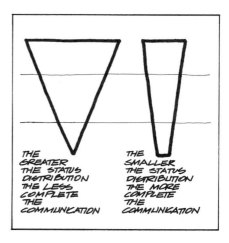

THE GREATER THE STATUS DISTRIBUTION THE LESS COMPLETE THE COMMUNICATION

THE SMALLER THE STATUS DISTRIBUTION THE MORE COMPLETE THE COMMUNICATION

LIST/VALUE OF COMPILED
STATUS SYMBOLS

ITEM	VALUE 1	2	3	4	5	6	7	8	9	10
⁞⁞⁞⁞			X							
⁞⁞⁞⁞							X			
⁞⁞⁞⁞					X					
⁞⁞⁞⁞									X	
⁞⁞⁞⁞		X								
⁞⁞⁞⁞				X						

LIST/DISTRIBUTION OF COMPILED
STATUS SYMBOLS

ITEM	NUMBER AT ORGANIZATION LEVEL 1	2	3	4	5
⁞⁞⁞⁞	20	4		3	
⁞⁞⁞⁞	7		3		1
⁞⁞⁞⁞		3		1	
⁞⁞⁞⁞	12	8	2		2
⁞⁞⁞⁞	13		7	5	4
⁞⁞⁞⁞	4	2	8		6

This necessitates either awarding equal status for positive and negative reports, or disassociating status rewards from reports altogether.

If the department chooses to define communication as any exchange of information or opinions between equals, then all individuals involved in communications should have equal or close-to-equal status, enabling them to interact freely and honestly. An argument in favor of distributing status evenly for purposes of communication is that the solution to a problem concerning a group of people is much more readily accepted by the group if its members have participated fully in developing the solution. User participation in problem solving also helps ensure that the solution developed is a viable one.

STATUS-SYMBOL ANALYSIS

If status-symbol distribution is to be planned and regulated in the office landscape, existing symbols must be identified and their distribution evaluated. Because social status is difficult to define and more difficult to control, the *status-symbol analysis* should be limited to material symbols. However, social status is too important to be overlooked, and the planners should make every effort to increase user awareness of its manifestations and ramifications.

The planning team should compile a complete list of existing status symbols and which department levels possess them. Each user group representative, in conjunction with her/his tally group, should then place a value of one to ten on each symbol listed. The average of the values assigned to any given item by each group becomes the final value for that item.

When this information has been gathered and calculated, it should be consolidated in a chart showing whether or not any given department level possesses a particular status symbol and what the value of that symbol is. The number of symbols for each department level, and their respective values, should be totaled separately and recorded beneath that level's column.

This information must be transferred to two graphs to be analyzed. These graphs are con-

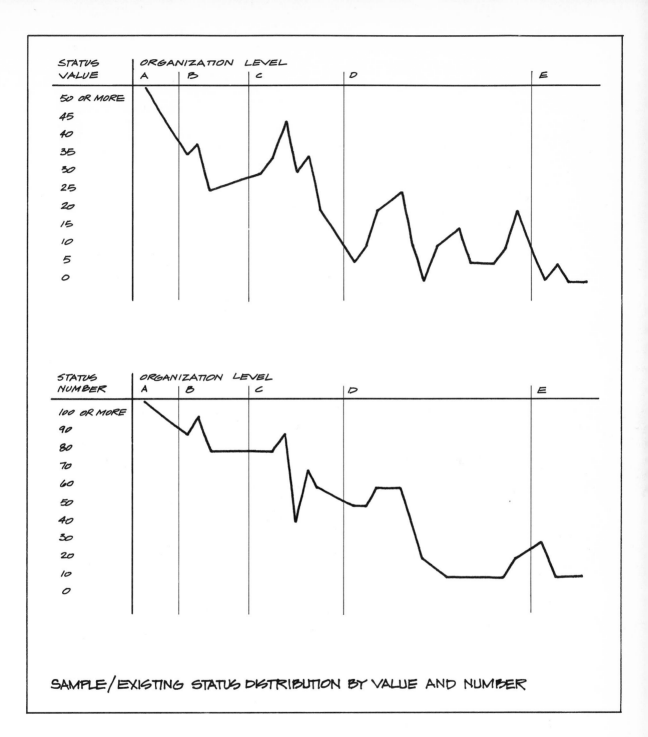

SAMPLE/EXISTING STATUS DISTRIBUTION BY VALUE AND NUMBER

STATUS VALUE OR NUMBER	ORGANIZATION LEVEL				
	A	B	C	D	E
10					
9					
8					
7					
6					
5					
4				IDEAL	
3					
2					
1					
0					

STATUS VALUE OR NUMBER	ORGANIZATION LEVEL				
	A	B	C	D	E
10					
9					
8					
7					
6					
5					
4					
3				ACCEPTABLE	
2					
1					
0					

SAMPLE / PLANNED STATUS DISTRIBUTION

structed alike, but one indicates existing status distribution by number, and the other by value. Departmental levels form the vertical dimension, and the range of totals of either the number of status symbols, or their values, form the horizontal. When the information is entered on the graphs under the correct levels and beside the correct totals, the department's existing material-status distribution becomes apparent, both in terms of quantity and quality. The graphs can then be compared, often showing that too many status symbols have developed within the department to be functional, and that they are distributed unevenly. The conclusions drawn from analyzing these charts form the planning basis for status redistribution and regulation.

PLANNING
STATUS DISTRIBUTION

Planning and moving into an open-landscape environment is an opportune time to revise status distribution. This does not mean all the old symbols are to be discarded, though their number should be drastically reduced. New symbols must be developed to replace old ones which would impair work flow in the landscape, but they must be economical, practical, and evenly distributed throughout department levels. In addition, a viable program of status distribution should be planned and established in order to avoid future reconversion to arbitrary, top-heavy status awards.

All status symbols used in the open plan must allow flexibility and workplace rearrangement. Flexibility is greatly impaired if even a few people are permitted oversized desks or closed offices. Closed offices are especially detrimental to the office landscape because they invariably and unnecessarily compromise the ideal communication and work-flow lines established in the correlation diagram.

To be functional, status should be redistributed evenly in any department or organization, but how equally it is distributed, in terms of value as well as number, is up to the planned-for department. Though one might like equality to become the rule rather than the exception, it is not. However, if equality, a straight horizontal line on both status-symbol analysis graphs,

OPEN
LANDSCAPE
STATUS
SYMBOLS
SHOULD BE
ECONOMICAL,
FUNCTIONAL, AND
EVENLY DISTRIBUTED

STATUS
SYMBOLS
MUST
ALLOW
FLEXIBILITY

SOME CONVENTIONAL
STATUS SYMBOLS
NO LONGER EXIST IN
THE OPEN LANDSCAPE

BOSS

OTHERS
BELONG TO EVERYONE

is ideal, then actual status redistribution should be as close to this as possible, a slightly diagonal line being the maximum variation acceptable.

The main point to remember in evaluating and planning status distribution is that the arbitrary, uncontrolled, imbalanced award of status symbols makes the search for status an end in itself, and status for status's sake becomes tyrannical, adversely affecting the individuals drawn into the competition and therefore the organization as a whole.

NOTE: *The following is a list of possible conventional symbols. Some of these, when carried over to the open-landscape plan, may become purely functional and not related to status at all.*

- *Private office*
- *Two-person office*
- *Office size*
- *Office location*
- *Office with or without windows*
- *Number of windows*
- *Name on office door*
- *Title on office door*
- *Desk size*
- *Desk-chair type*
- *Furniture type—luxury, standard*
- *Private conference room*
- *Conference table in office*
- *Informal conference area in office*
- *Private washroom*
- *Carpeted office*
- *Carpet type*
- *Special curtains or drapes*
- *Special wall colors and/or finishes*
- *Kinds of decorative and/or art objects*
- *Plants*
- *Bookcase*
- *Bookcase type*
- *Credenza*
- *Bar and/or refrigerator*
- *Water pitcher*
- *Telephone via switchboard*
- *Telephone via secretary*
- *Private telephone line*
- *Private secretary*
- *Shared secretary*

- *Private reception area*
- *Personal letterhead*
- *Personal business cards provided by the organization*
- *Key to washroom*
- *Club memberships paid for by the organization*
- *Paid professional memberships*
- *Inclusion on in-office periodical-distribution list*
- *Credit cards furnished by the organization*
- *Expense account*
- *Expense-account type*
- *Flexible working hours*
- *Special vacation privileges*
- *Participation in management conferences*
- *Name on building and/or floor directory*
- *Private parking space*
- *Parking-space location*
- *Car provided by the organization*
- *Type of car provided*

Section Seven

Color
and
Graphics

C olor and graphics in the open office landscape should be selected and/or designed very carefully. Because a large number of people are to be working in the same area, it is critical to consider the physical and psychological effects of different colors. Blues, for example, cause people's pulse rates to decrease and they perspire less than they ordinarily might. Reds, on the other hand, have an opposite effect, and greens and grays are neutral. Most people find autumn colors most comfortable and easy to live with over extended periods of time.

Color choices must not be arbitrary, but planned and balanced. A color scheme should be developed for the department as a whole, with particular attention to balancing group work areas. Although the colors selected for individual workplaces are certainly important, they should be considered in the larger context of the group, discounting the possibility of each user choosing his/her favorite color. This would undoubtedly cause the overall scheme to be unbalanced, thereby affecting the open environment adversely.

Graphics, like color, should be fully integrated with the landscape, and should not merely be decorative, but functional as well. They must identify, inform, or direct. Graphics might be used to identify a particular activity, indicate its location, and/or direct people to it. But isolated blocks of color, symbols, or other figures that do not serve a function within the office are decoration, not graphics.

Within the scope of this definition, almost anything can become graphics. Plants, paintings, sculpture, letters, numbers, symbols—all could be part of the graphic scheme if used to identify, inform, or direct.

For example, upon entering the landscape area, a visitor might find a directory of the department. Each group within the department might be represented by a symbol, number, letter, block of color, etc. The graphic representation of that group then could be repeated and used to direct the visitor to its location. Further, graphics might be used to identify the functions of groups or employees. The status or position of different individuals also might be represented by graphic symbols. For instance, all division heads within the organization might be identified with a block of

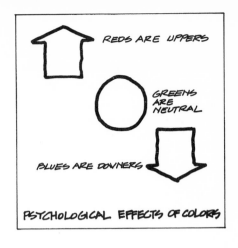

REDS ARE UPPERS

GREENS ARE NEUTRAL

BLUES ARE DOWNERS

PSYCHOLOGICAL EFFECTS OF COLORS

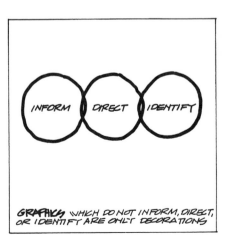

INFORM   DIRECT   IDENTIFY

GRAPHICS WHICH DO NOT INFORM, DIRECT, OR IDENTIFY ARE ONLY DECORATIONS

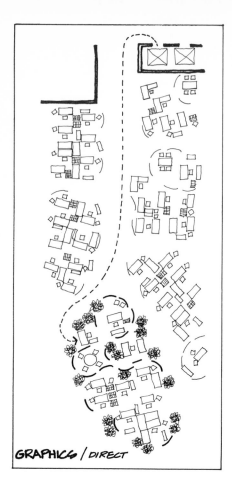

GRAPHICS / DIRECT

GRAPHICS / DIRECT

color at their workplaces. A more subtle form of status identification might be to add more, larger, or different kinds of plants than those used for other employees.

Art can also define areas and express status. A piece of sculpture, for example, might turn or terminate a circulation route. Paintings might identify the status of a group or individual, as well as define areas. When used in such a manner, both are graphics.

Through the use of graphics, the department, group, or individual can acquire a unique personality and identity. A well-planned and integrated graphic scheme can visually enhance the office landscape environment and can serve as a functional subelement in the office. But no matter how colorful and aesthetically sound, to be effective, graphics must have a purpose. If tossed together and scattered about carelessly, they become confusing and disruptive.

One pitfall to be avoided in using graphics is tying them to the office hardware, such as desks, chairs, and bookcases. Graphics and furniture, although they may complement each other, serve different functions. If a desk or chair is used as part of a graphic scheme, it then must remain as an integral part of the scheme and cannot be moved into other areas. This decreases the flexibility of both the graphic scheme and the furniture and furnishings.

NOTE: *Here are some additional considerations for the selection and/or design of color and graphics in the open landscape:*

■ *A pleasant environment should be provided the entire office staff, eliminating possible competition for better space.*

■ *A monotonous office environment should be avoided because the environment directly relates to the employees' attitudes toward their work.*

■ *The environment should be stimulating, but should not cause stress or antagonize the users. A mixture of colors is suggested, with slightly more of the red than the blue spectrum.*

■ *Extreme light/dark contrasts should be avoided. Colors selected for the open landscape should be harmonious, with distinction at close range, but blending at a distance.*

■ *Exaggerated or super graphics, if used, should be*

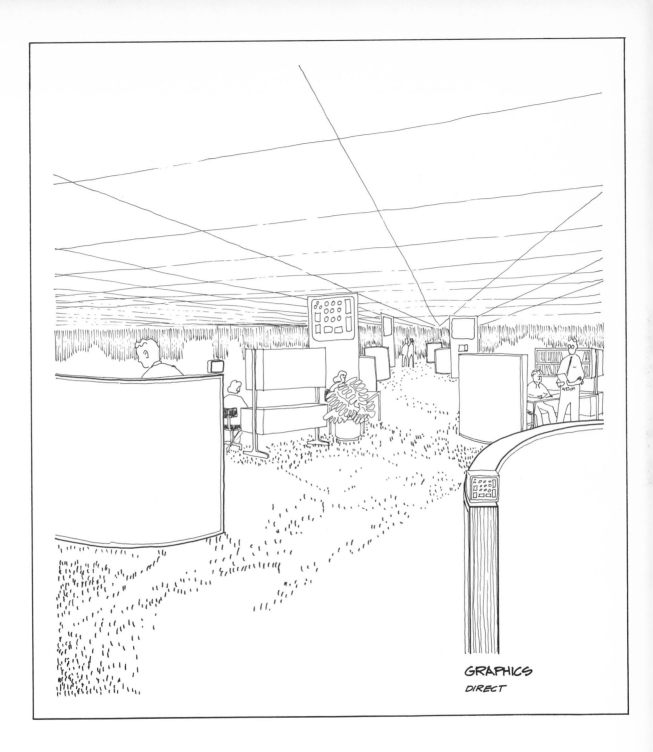

GRAPHICS
DIRECT

GRAPHICS / INFORM

GRAPHICS / IDENTIFY

carefully planned, designed, and placed to avoid becoming tiresome to the users.

■ *Columns and power and signal poles should blend with their surroundings and not be emphasized.*

■ *The carpet should be light-reflective to permit the white or off-white ceiling to pick up a very slight color tint.*

■ *The carpet should be nondirectional, with either no pattern, or a small, slight one. Large patterns and directional designs optically oppose workplace arrangements.*

■ *Autumn colors are suggested for carpets. Black or other dark colors, and pale blues and greens have either a dulling or sleep-provoking effect on the users.*

■ *Desk and other work surfaces should be light in color, to avoid high contrast with work papers. Light woods (oak, birch, ash) are recommended over dark ones (walnut, teak, rosewood) where wooden furniture is used.*

■ *Floor entries/exits and traffic lanes should not be emphasized by color variations which will hinder future workplace rearrangements.*

■ *The open landscape should have a comprehensive color scheme. If more than one floor is involved, each floor may have color scheme variations provided they do not prohibit between-floor furniture interchanges.*

■ *Because lounges are somewhat separate from the general open-landscape area and serve a different function, colors for lounge furniture and furnishings should deviate from the overall color scheme.*

■ *Graphics must identify, inform, or direct.*

■ *Graphics should not be integral parts of furniture and furnishings, or the flexibility of both graphics and furniture is compromised.*

■ *Graphics including persons' names and/or titles should be designed to permit these names and/or titles to be changed easily.*

The Open-Landscape Layout

O pen plans are considered confusing and arbitrary by many people. Though it may be true that they appear confusing to first-time visitors because they are unfamiliar, well-designed open landscapes are neither confusing nor arbitrary. But, they are drastically different from traditional offices and do require initial adjustment by both users and visitors. This is not peculiar to office landscapes; a certain amount of learning and unlearning goes with almost any change from the conventional to the unconventional.

Behind each well-designed open landscape, there is logic and orderliness. This section is intended to describe the approach necessary to achieve a functional, flexible, and orderly landscape layout.

OPEN
LANDSCAPE
MUST
BE
LOGICAL AND
ORDERLY

ZONE FORMATION

The correlation diagram, backed by workplace types and sizes, determines the space needed for the entire department as well as the space needs and ideal relationships of each of its groups and related special areas. *Zone formation* is essentially the application of the correlation diagram to the facility plan.

By this phase of the project, the facility plan should have been designed to meet—in so far as site limitations permit—the criteria established in the correlation diagram. And the planning team should have planned the floor distribution of tally groups according to quantity and quality of interaction, again compromising the correlation diagram as little as possible. Now, the zone formations, which show the arrangement of groups on each floor, should be laid out on the new facility floor plans, representing groups as adjacent, straight-edged bubbles—round-cornered if desirable. Each bubble must be to scale; that is, it must represent, accurately, the number of square feet allocated the corresponding group. It is critical for the bubbles to be exactly to scale.

The zone formation is fairly easy to lay out; however, several things are worth noting. First, while the bubbles must touch, they cannot overlap. Second, the bubbles should be kept as fat or squarish as possible; but, because major corridors should not be perpendicular or parallel to each other, and because they are best located between, not through, group areas, the

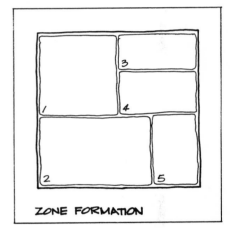

ZONE FORMATION

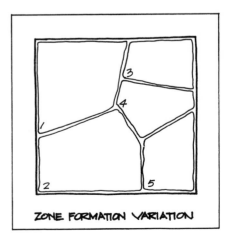

ZONE FORMATION VARIATION

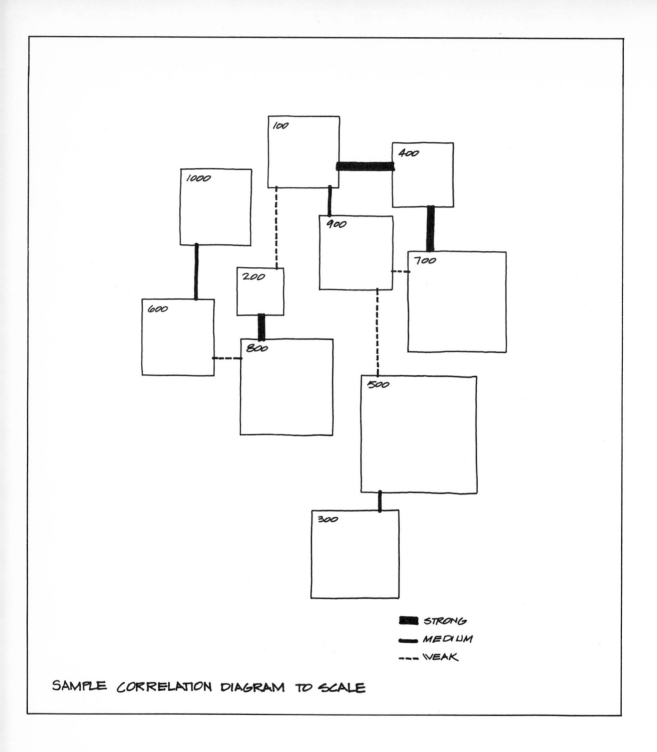

SAMPLE CORRELATION DIAGRAM TO SCALE

■■■ STRONG
━━ MEDIUM
--- WEAK

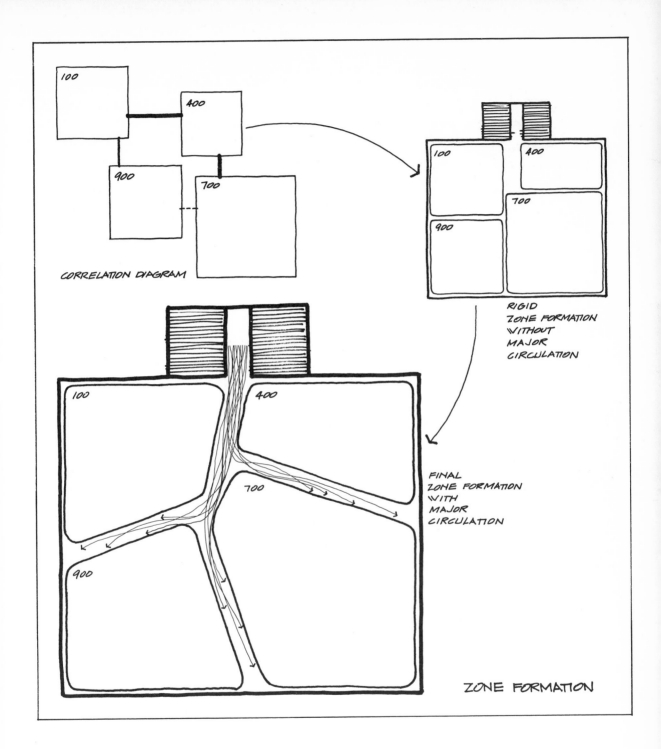

CORRELATION DIAGRAM

RIGID
ZONE FORMATION
WITHOUT
MAJOR
CIRCULATION

FINAL
ZONE FORMATION
WITH
MAJOR
CIRCULATION

ZONE FORMATION

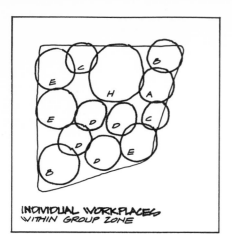

INDIVIDUAL WORKPLACES WITHIN GROUP ZONE

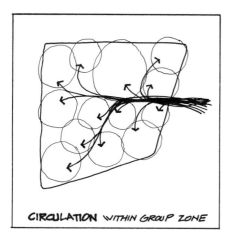

CIRCULATION WITHIN GROUP ZONE

bubbles cannot form true squares or rectangles. Third, zone formations for each floor will differ simply because group sizes, numbers, and relationships vary.

NOTE: *The zone formations in the accompanying illustrations indicate possible variations within the framework of a constant floor plan.*

The zone-formation layouts should be presented to and discussed with all members of the department. They should be reviewed first by the planning team, then by the users through the user group representatives. Probably few changes will be suggested for the zone formations because they are based on the previously discussed and approved correlation diagram, but this review session is the first opportunity the department's staff and management will have had to see their groups' locations in the new landscape.

LAYOUT LOGIC

After the zone formation has been completed for each floor, the layout of individual workplaces and group equipment areas is accomplished one group at a time. Then adjustments and alterations are made to produce a workable layout for the floor as a whole. The group layout is developed by indicating individual workplaces and shared equipment areas by circles drawn within the group's space as designated in the zone formation. The size and placement of these circles is determined by the information included on the appropriate tally group intra-action sheet, Section Three. Based on the square footages previously calculated for workplace standards, this intra-action sheet shows each individual's required workplace type to scale, as well as group equipment needs. In addition, the sheet indicates the users' ideal in-group relationships.

As a group's layout is being developed, it is advantageous to consider just how major floor circulation will relate to the given work group. The designer must decide where major floor circulation will enter the group area and, further, how circulation within the group will be handled. Preliminary circulation routes may be represented by colored lines, making sure that the access to one individual does not interfere with another's workplace. No workplace should be ap-

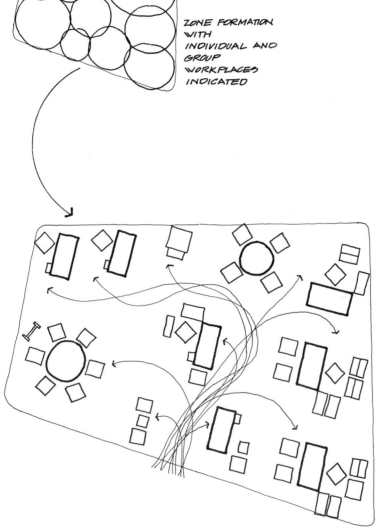

GROUP LAYOUT

ZONE FORMATION
WITH
INDIVIDUAL AND
GROUP
WORKPLACES
INDICATED

INDIVIDUAL
WORKPLACE
LAYOUT
WITH
CIRCULATION BUT
WITHOUT
SCREENS AND
PLANTERS

NEVER ENTER WORKPLACE FROM REAR

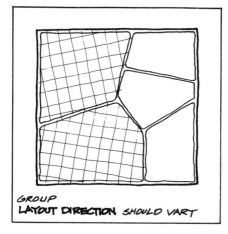

GROUP LAYOUT DIRECTION SHOULD VARY

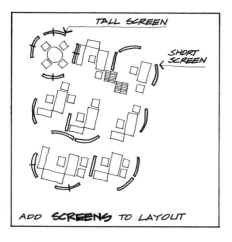

ADD SCREENS TO LAYOUT

proached from the rear, and both in-group and major circulation lines should be as short as possible.

In order to avoid unnecessary layout reworking, it is advisable to verify both individual workplace and shared-equipment locations within all groups, and major and minor circulation patterns with the planning team before adding furniture and equipment to the layout. Reviewing the layout before it becomes too detailed also makes it easier to evaluate the overall open-landscape arrangement for the given floor.

Once the preliminary workplace and circulation layouts are approved by the planning team and the users, the designer may add furniture and shared equipment. This requires further reference to the tally group intra-action sheets, each of which graphically illustrates its group's equipment and each item of furniture to be included in a given workplace. The furniture and equipment simply need to be arranged in the appropriate circles. Probably most workplace types were originally designed as rectangles, and so a few adjustments may be necessary to adapt them to the circles.

A major criterion for furniture and group equipment arrangement is that all workplaces within a given group be parallel. This does not mean, however, that all group members must face the same way; they may face opposing directions. Meeting this criterion is simplified by overlaying a 90-degree grid on the group area. This grid also enables the designer to ensure the proximity of workplaces and telephone and electrical outlets, and to arrange a few workplaces at right angles to the majority if this is absolutely necessary. Parallel workplace arrangement within each group maximizes the user's feeling of spaciousness, and, because the workplaces of one group are not parallel to those of adjacent groups, it also helps create a group subjective space.

The final step in the layout is arranging the visual/acoustical screens, and plants and planters. There are no set numbers of screens needed for individuals or groups, though one or two per workplace is typical. The only criterion is to provide privacy for the users, remembering that when a screen is located between two workplaces, it serves both. Tall screens

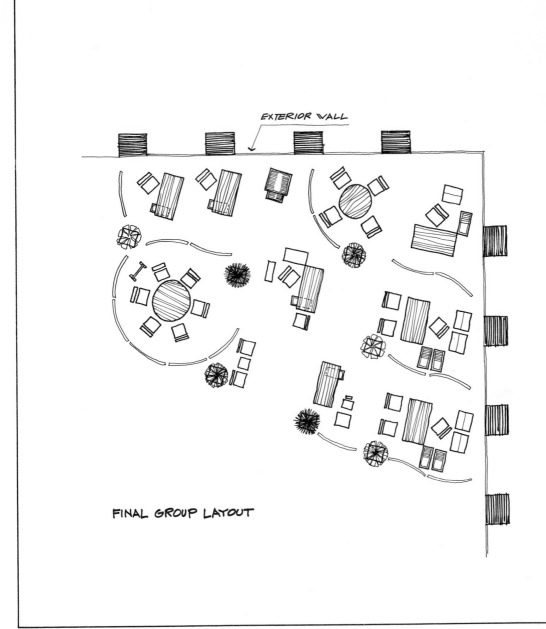

EXTERIOR WALL

FINAL GROUP LAYOUT

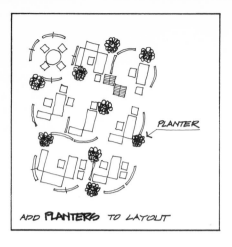

ADD **PLANTERS** TO LAYOUT

PRESENTATION MODEL

3-DIMENSIONAL
WORKING MODEL

should be used sparingly, and are usually required only around conference areas.

NOTE: *It is much easier to add a few screens after move-in than to remove them once in use.*

Probably plants cause fewer arguments when used to identify status than when they define transportation corridors and workplaces, their most common usages. Employees tend to form strong personal attachments to plants defining their work areas and adjacent corridors. While possibly psychologically satisfying, such affection causes problems when work spaces are rearranged and individuals moved. People want to take *their* plants with them, which means that the boundaries of corridors or workplaces go also. Seldom does logic, wheedling, or threatening convince them that the plants in their arms are parts of corridors and not theirs.

In spite of user possessiveness toward them, however, plants and planters do provide partial visual privacy and work well as corridor definers. When deciding where to place the plants in the layout, the designer should keep in mind that they afford only visual, not acoustical, privacy. The average number of planters in the open landscape is usually about one per workplace.

USE OF MODELS

In many open-landscape projects, models are used as design/layout and presentation tools. There are basically three types: a detailed presentation model, a three-dimensional working model, and a two-dimensional working model.

The presentation model is used primarily for review purposes. It is a scaled-down replica of a given space, including furniture and furnishings, colors, textures, etc.; however, because of the time and expense involved in constructing the model, it usually represents only a small portion of the overall landscape.

Although this model is indispensable for study and review, it also provides the users with a wonderfully realistic picture of the open environment and individual workplaces. In addition, a model scope can be used to bring the model into scale with the viewer, and, when attached to a camera, can make photographs of the model look as if they were taken of the actual facility.

NOTE: *Most architectural, interior design, and office landscape planning firms either have their own model shops or have access to model builders. Also, some furniture manufacturers provide scaled-down versions of their products for use in models. Presentation models are expensive, but they are far less expensive than building full-scale mock-ups and are, for all practical purposes, just as enlightening.*

The three-dimensional working model simply has fewer details than the presentation model. For example, a desk might be represented by a three-dimensional block constructed to scale. The two-dimensional model is also fairly undetailed, but shows the space and furniture to scale only in plan, that is, from above. Vertical dimensions are not considered. This model may be constructed of plastic, paper board, or even paper, and is consequently quite inexpensive.

Both three- and two-dimensional models serve the same purpose: to eliminate costly drafting and provide the designer with working tools which permit fast, accurate layouts. Adjustments and rearrangements can be accomplished quickly with these models, and either the models themselves, if the pieces are fixed, or photographs of the models can serve as blueprints for proper furniture positioning, service outlet locations, etc. In short, working models replace layout drawings.

If working models are used for layout design, it is advantageous to have background boards to scale for each floor, indicating stairs, elevators, columns, service outlets, and/or any other elements which vary from floor to floor. It is also worth noting that, because layout design is time-consuming and therefore expensive, most planners postpone final layouts until just before move-in. This also simplifies making last-minute changes.

2-DIMENSIONAL WORKING MODEL

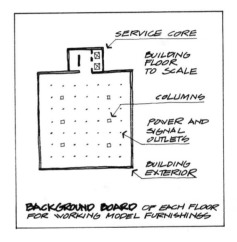

SERVICE CORE

BUILDING FLOOR TO SCALE

COLUMNS

POWER AND SIGNAL OUTLETS

BUILDING EXTERIOR

BACKGROUND BOARD OF EACH FLOOR FOR WORKING MODEL FURNISHINGS

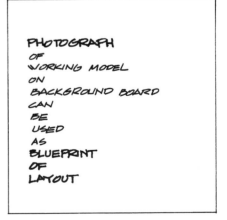

PHOTOGRAPH OF WORKING MODEL ON BACKGROUND BOARD CAN BE USED AS BLUEPRINT OF LAYOUT

Section Nine

Move-in and Follow-up

Move-in and Follow-up

The move into a new or renovated space should be handled as a planning task in order to disrupt the work processes of the department as little as possible. If carefully thought out, *move-in* can usually be accomplished over a weekend, taking only a few hours of the users' time to pack and tag files and materials for the movers, and to unpack them in the new space.

It is important to arrange for power and signal equipment installation well ahead of time and, because of the probable complexity of the system, to include telephone company representatives in the move-in planning. In addition, coordinators should be appointed by the planning team to oversee the move and ensure that all goes smoothly. Usually, the members of the user group function well as coordinators because they are in close touch with the members of their tally groups. There should also be a general coordinator, most often a member of both the planning team and the department. Theoretically, the coordinators should run furniture and layout checks prior to move-in. However, if time does not permit, this may be postponed until follow-up.

Follow-up essentially involves assessing the open-landscape environment to determine both the adjustments that may be necessary to achieve the planned results, and employee attitudes. The conclusions developed are included in two separate evaluation reports which are intended to inform management of follow-up findings and to function as guidelines for future planning.

Immediately after move-in, a *physical and environmental evaluation* should be undertaken. This requires precise measurement and observation, and is primarily a job for specialists, although the planning team working group should determine whether any workplaces or group areas are slightly too tight or too open and make whatever adjustments may be required. The appropriate specialists should measure and assess the adequacy and evenness of the lighting; the efficiency of the air-conditioning system related to air flow, humidity, rate of exchange, and overall temperature control; and the acoustical balance of the space. The acoustical evaluation is the most complex of these, requiring precise measurement of the sound-absorbing capacities of visual/acoustical screens,

MOVE-IN
MUST
BE
PLANNED
∴
MOVE-IN
IS A
PLANNING
TASK

FOR
FAST AND
EASY
MOVE-IN
PACK AND TAG
MATERIALS
FOR
FLOOR,
GROUP, AND
WORKPLACE
DESTINATION

PHYSICAL AND
ENVIRONMENTAL
EVALUATION
MEASURES
SUCCESS
OF
APPLIED
PLANNING
THEORIES

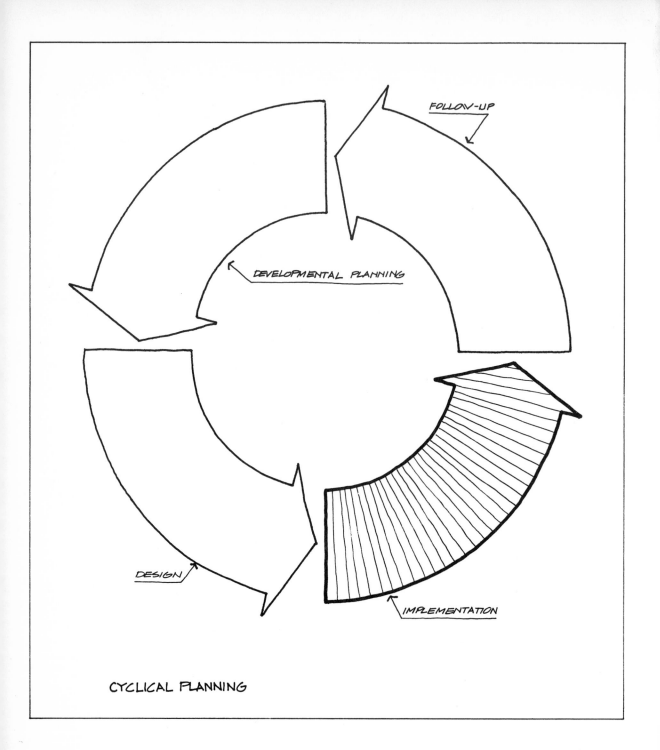

FOLLOW-UP

DEVELOPMENTAL PLANNING

DESIGN

IMPLEMENTATION

CYCLICAL PLANNING

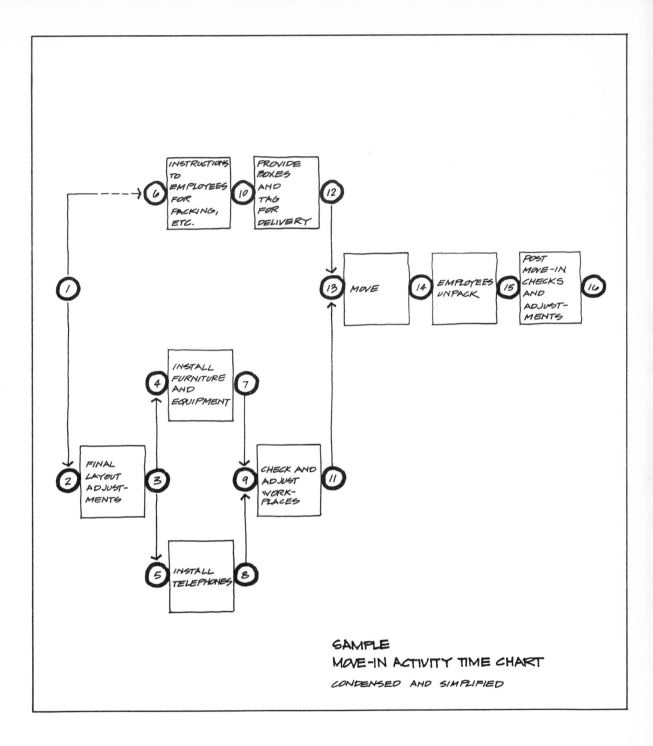

SAMPLE
MOVE-IN ACTIVITY TIME CHART
CONDENSED AND SIMPLIFIED

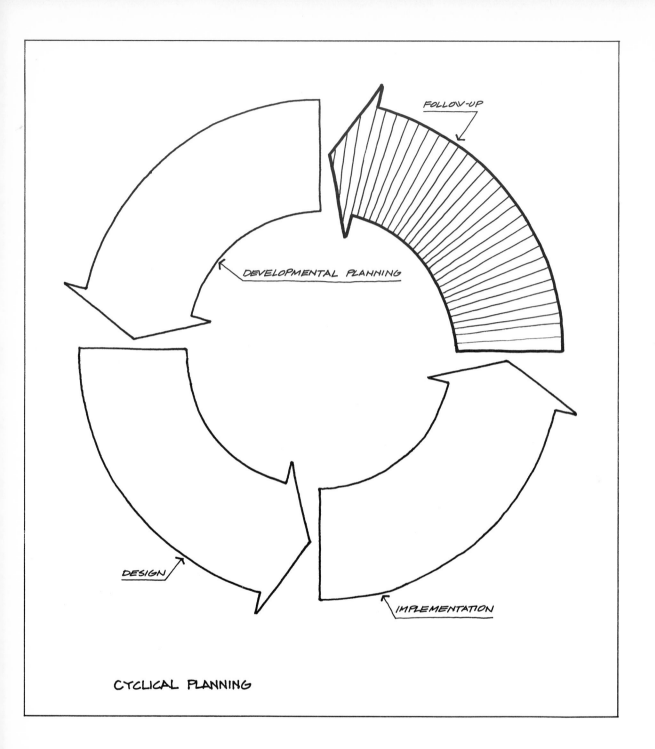

FOLLOW-UP

DEVELOPMENTAL PLANNING

IMPLEMENTATION

DESIGN

CYCLICAL PLANNING

QUESTION	RESULT

F/ DO YOU FEEL THAT YOUR OWN INDIVIDUAL NEEDS, AS RELATED TO THE PERFORMANCE OF YOUR JOB, WERE ADEQUATELY TAKEN INTO CONSIDERATION IN THE DEVELOPMENT AND FINAL LAYOUT OF YOUR WORKPLACE?

DEFINITELY YES	78 %
PARTIALLY	18
DEFINITELY NO	4

G/ DOES THE PHYSICAL LAYOUT OF YOUR WORK ENVIRONMENT MAKE YOU FEEL YOU ARE:

A MEMBER OF A TEAM	94 %
A SOLITARY WORKER	4
ISOLATED	2

H/ DOES THE PHYSICAL LAYOUT OF YOUR WORKPLACE MAKE YOU FEEL THAT IT IS DIFFICULT TO MAINTAIN YOUR IDENTITY?

YES	2 %
PARTIALLY	4
NO	94

I/ HOW DOES THE ARRANGEMENT OF WORKPLACES IN YOUR AREA AFFECT CONTACTS WITH PEOPLE YOU WORK MOST FREQUENTLY WITH?

GREATLY ASSISTS	82 %
SLIGHTLY ASSISTS	6
MAKES NO DIFFERENCE	8
SLIGHTLY INTERFERES	0
GREATLY INTERFERES	4

	ALWAYS	FREQUENTLY	SOMETIMES	SELDOM	NEVER
J/ DO YOU FIND YOURSELF INTERFERING WITH OTHERS BECAUSE OF THE WAY THE SPACE IS ARRANGED?	3	0	9	81	7
K/ DO OTHERS INTERFERE WITH YOUR WORK BECAUSE OF THE ARRANGEMENT OF SPACE?	0	5	16	64	15
L/ ARE THE MATERIALS YOU MOST FREQUENTLY NEED IMMEDIATELY AVAILABLE?	13	43	26	9	8

PARTIAL SUMMARY OF ATTITUDE SURVEY

blinds, carpet, and ceiling as arranged and/or installed in the space. Acoustical measurements should be taken of all workplace types to calculate the privacy they afford; then these figures should be compared with measurements taken of the previous conventional office types. Usually, these comparisons show that the acoustical privacy of the open landscape exceeds that of the conventional office. In addition, the background sound system should be tuned by the acoustical specialist while users are in the space so that the proper background sound level can be established.

Three to four weeks after move-in, the working group and an appropriate specialist should conduct an *employee attitude survey.* A questionnaire should be designed which encompasses all elements of the open-landscape environment—psychological, physical, and functional—including but certainly not limited to the following: workplace location, group location, access to people and information, effectiveness and productivity, identity, status, visual and acoustical privacy, lighting and temperature, furniture and equipment, special facilities, filing system, plants, and color and graphics. This questionnaire should be distributed to all users, and should allow a range of answers to each question in order to register degrees of positive and negative feelings.

The results of the employee attitude survey should be summarized in graphic and written form and, in addition to the findings of the physical and environmental evaluation, should be included in an evaluation report.

Approximately six months after move-in, a similar employee attitude survey should be conducted and summarized in a second report. The purpose of the two surveys is to analyze the users' immediate and postadjustment responses to the open landscape, and to compare the two. Usually, the initial responses are positive and the second are even more so. The surveys are also helpful in pinpointing any adjustments that need to be made.

Follow-up does not mark the end of the planning but the end of the first cycle. The in-house working group members should continue applying the office landscape approach, though perhaps on a smaller

EMPLOYEE ATTITUDE SURVEY SHOULD COVER PSYCHOLOGICAL, PHYSICAL, AND FUNCTIONAL ASPECTS OF THE OPEN-PLAN ENVIRONMENT

SURVEY QUESTIONS SHOULD ALLOW A RANGE OF ANSWERS

scale, to detect and plan for needed adjustments and rearrangements in the landscape. This is of the utmost importance because the landscape must continue to reflect and accommodate changing individual and group tasks, and departmental expansion.

NOTE: *Follow-up planning is not unique to open-landscape installations; it should, in fact, be the rule in every organization regardless of office type. Yet in the conventional office, layout adjustments are usually postponed until the situation reaches a crisis stage because of the time, cost, and work disruption involved in rearranging floor-to-ceiling partitions and conventional furniture.*

Numerous studies have been conducted concerning the cost differences between altering conventional and open-landscape offices. The results varied, depending on extent of alterations, type of partitions, geographical location, etc., of each organization studied, but in every instance the cost of alterations was far less for the open landscape than for the conventional office. The costs for open landscapes ranged astoundingly from 0.8 to 11.2 percent of the costs of conventional offices, and averaged about 3.0 percent. Cost comparisons were made on a square foot basis, which was to the advantage of the conventional office because it is generally about 15 percent larger than a comparable open landscape. A more accurate comparison would be between workplaces, but the data for this are scarce.

The point here is that follow-up and cyclical planning for the landscape are quite inexpensive, especially when improved work flow, communication, and productivity are considered.

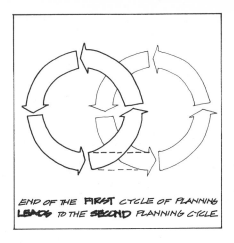

END OF THE **FIRST** CYCLE OF PLANNING **LEADS** TO THE **SECOND** PLANNING CYCLE

CONVENTIONAL VERSUS OPEN LANDSCAPE

THE COST OF ALTERATION

Section Ten

Intangibles

M ost advantages of the office landscape are measurable; however, there are quite a few, confirmed by open-landscape users over the course of many projects, that are very real but intangible, that is, difficult to measure. Some of these intangible benefits are listed below.

- The landscape is a more pleasant and stimulating work environment than the conventional office, and affects efficiency and productivity positively.
- Communication and work flow between individuals and groups are improved.
- Work flow and communication inefficiencies are easier to detect and rectify.
- Access to individuals, groups, and information is easier and faster.
- A feeling of group identity is created or bolstered, and individual and group morale is higher.
- Because they are no longer in individual cubicles or offices, the users often work in small teams, taking advantage of each other's knowledge, ideas, and fresh points of view.
- The openness of and user visibility within the landscape cause the users to become more considerate of one another.
- Possibly because of close identification with the space itself, and because it is aesthetically pleasing, the users tend to improve their personal grooming.
- By the same token, individual workplaces are also more orderly than in the conventional office.
- The organization's overall image to visitors and business associates is enhanced.
- Absenteeism and abuse of sick leave are reduced.
- Personnel turnover is reduced and recruiting new personnel is easier.
- Department transfers and new employees adjust more quickly and easily to their new positions because of user accessibility and openness of communication.
- The users understand and appreciate the landscape because of their participation in its planning and design.
- There is less verticality in the organization's structure and hierarchy.
- User relationships and interactions become closer and less formalized because communication lines are more open and equal.

■ The users' self-esteem and security grow and are supported by more open communication and an equitable, nonarbitrary status distribution program.

■ The users feel more esteemed by their colleagues because their accomplishments are more visible. This, and a growing sense of individuality and identity, causes the users to take more pride in their work, then to be more esteemed, etc., so that an upward spiral results from the mutual reinforcement of self-esteem, esteem by colleagues, and productivity.

■ The users' pride in and identification with the organization are also renewed and strengthened, perhaps because by planning and implementing an office landscape the organization has shown itself to be progressive and interested in its personnel as well as efficiency.

■ User complaints, most commonly directed at management, are almost eliminated. This may be due, at least in part, to the close proximity and accessibility of management to other users.

■ Increased user/management interaction fortifies mutual esteem.

■ Accessibility, visibility, and open communication lines allow management to pinpoint group members of real value to the organization, and to put these employees' talents to the best uses. For example, if it becomes apparent to a supervisor that a given employee is especially talented in an area she/he is not primarily involved in, then the supervisor can change the employee's tasks and involvement accordingly. This is good for both the organization and the individual, and probably would not be a possibility without employee/management familiarity. This familiarity also enables management to identify any employees who are altogether unproductive.

■ The office landscape facilitates faster, more informed decision making. Mutual accessibility, proximity to group activities, and informal communication which encourages negative as well as positive reports combine to make more complete information available to management when decisions are needed.

Perspective

Conceiving of the organization as a machine which must be well planned and designed to run efficiently has become a cliché, and it becomes a dangerous one when the organization's employees are seen as machine parts. The office is a tool for the use of those working within it, not the other way around. This is a simple, obvious point, but one surprisingly easy for management to lose sight of, or the employee as automaton would not itself have become a clichéd notion. There are no laws to protect the employee's sense of individuality and identity, and so the emphasis placed on the employee's psychological as well as physical well-being is finally up to management. The organization needs and expects a great deal from its employees in terms of energy, talent, and dependability, and, in return, it would seem to be a sound idea for the organization to invest some of its resources in its people, over and above salaries.

Although many of these investments should result in tangible benefits for the organization and its employees, some very important ones are intangible. If the organization is structured less hierarchically than is traditional, allowing close, fully communicative relationships between employees and management instead of strict report-and-command lines, then employees are free, in fact encouraged, to take on extraordinary responsibility and to suggest and test innovations. This increases the employees' sense of individuality and self-esteem as well as job involvement and productivity, which cannot but be beneficial to the organization. However, because communication occurs between individuals, open communication cannot be programmed. It must be allowed and nurtured by a secure management to whom it is unnecessary to make employees feel ill at ease, whether by displaying social status or threatening employees with loss of status.

Personnel salaries should be the maximum the organization can afford, rather than the minimum it can get away with. In addition, all salaries should be made public within the company, and should be standardized with regard to positions and position levels in order to avoid driving wedges between employees of the same rank. For the same reason, merit rewards should be unconnected to raises. Bonuses, for example, given for accomplishing difficult tasks are easily understood by other employees because the rewards are for specific successes.

Individuals' freedom and eagerness to assume responsibility can also be strengthened by flexible working hours and/or a four-day week. Although many management-level personnel believe these measures decrease productivity, this is rarely the case. On the contrary, productivity often increases because employee morale goes up. Further, employees should be allowed to accumulate vacation time or to split it into small segments if they prefer, rather than being forced to use the allotted two or three weeks at one time during the year or lose them altogether.

In terms of benefits, the organization should set up profit sharing and pension plans for its employees. A group health insurance plan, including disability, should be paid for by the organization, and other group plans, such as life and auto insurance, should be made available through the company to enable employees to pay lower rates. Pregnant women, in accordance with the guidelines established by the U.S. Department of Labor, should not lose their jobs after a few months' pregnancy, but should be allowed to work until they themselves decide to take a temporary leave of absence. A certain number of weeks of this leave should be covered by the organization's disability insurance plan, and these women should, upon their return, continue in their previous positions.

Nepotism rules should also be rethought. Often, rules are established which bar nepotism regardless of the circumstances. For example, a wife and husband might be prohibited from working in the same organization even though their tasks would be entirely separate in kind and in location. At their worst, these rules can prohibit a wife or husband from working and permit a son or daughter to become a regular employee. It is unfortunate that, in most such cases, a wife is prohibited and a son allowed, and the problem becomes one not only of inconsistent rules, but also of sexism.

The organization should also provide facilities, such as day-care and recreation centers, which meet employee needs. The day-care center must be open to the children of both male and female employees. It is not expensive to furnish a day-care center, and the benefits it provides for employees are great. A recreation center, for women and men, serves much the same purpose as employee lounges, enabling personnel to change environments. Physical exercise also helps people feel physically well, thereby aiding job productivity and effectiveness.

In addition to providing benefits and services for its employees, the organization should plan carefully its impact on the community. Often, the organization can benefit both its employees and the community simultaneously. For example, the company can provide a transportation system for its employees and, by doing so, help reduce community traffic and pollution problems. If the organization builds a new facility, this facility can supply its users with an optimum working environment and enhance the surrounding area aesthetically. The company can also maintain healthy community relations by allowing extraorganizational groups to use its meeting rooms and/or auditorium during off-hours.

It is hoped that the primary point made in these discussions of benefits is that the organization, regardless of size, has a responsibility to the employee and the community. The reasons for fulfilling this responsibility are not based entirely on goodwill and generosity, but also relate to the effective functioning of the organization.

It is crucial for the organization to attract and maintain talented, enthusiastic personnel, and to avoid a high turnover rate requiring that a great deal of time and money be spent on recruiting and training employees. If an employee loses a sense of worth and individuality, then the chances are that his/her commitment to and involvement in the organization will be minimal, and turnover, in general, will be high. If, on the other hand, he/she feels esteemed by colleagues and maintains independence and self-esteem, then the employee is much more likely to be of real value to the organization, whatever his/her position or level.

Bibliography

Adams, S.: "Status Congruency as a Variable in Small Group Performance," *Social Forces,* no. 36, October 1953.

Bennis, Warren G.: "Everything You Always Wanted to Know about Change," *Environment/Planning and Design,* Summer 1971.

Bullens, Harry, Wolfgang Eckardt, and Michael K. Nathan: "Problems of Planning, Organization, and Leadership (in Hospitals)," *Kommunikation,* vol. 5, no. 4, June 1969.

Canally, Richard J.: *Office Landscape Report,* Administrative Management Society, Willow Grove, Pennsylvania, June 1972.

An Employee Guide, Mercedes-Benz of North America, Fort Lee, New Jersey, August 1972.

Ergonomics in the Design of Office Furniture, Industrial Medicine, vol. 38, no. 4, April 1969.

Facilities Planning Report to the Southwest Educational Development Laboratories, Southwest Educational Development Laboratories, Austin, Texas, May 17, 1971.

Fleishman, Edwin A.: *Studies in Personnel and Industrial Psychology,* Dorsey Press, Homewood, Illinois, 1961.

Hamme, Richard, and Don Huggins: "Acoustics in the Open Plan," *Office Design,* July 1968.

Hepner, Harry W.: *Perceptive Management and Supervision,* Prentice-Hall, Englewood Cliffs, New Jersey, 1961.

Kahn, Robert L.: "Productivity and Job Satisfaction," *Personnel Psychology,* Autumn 1960.

"Making Office Walls Come Tumbling Down," *Business Week,* May 11, 1968.

Miner, John B.: *The Management of Ineffective Performance,* McGraw-Hill, New York, 1963.

The ODCASO Office Evaluation Report, U.S. Department of Labor and General Services Administration, Washington, D.C., February 1971.

The ODCASO Office Landscape Planning Report, U.S. Department of Labor and General Services Administration, Washington, D.C., 1969.

Office Landscape: A Feasibility Study, U.S. Department of Labor and General Services Administration, Washington, D.C., 1968.

The Office Landscape: A Report on User Experience, Administrative Management Society, Willow Grove, Pennsylvania, December 13, 1971.

"Office Landscaping," *Skyscraper Management,* December 1968.

"The Office That Changes Gracefully," *Office Design,* July 1968.

Palmer, Alvin E.: "Graphics in the Landscape," *Office Design,* May 1969.

Parsons, T., and E. A. Shills: *Towards a General Theory of Action,* Harvard University Press, Cambridge, Massachusetts, 1951.

Pile, John: "Clearing the Mystery of the 'Office Landscape' or 'Bürolandschaft,'" *Interiors,* January 1968.

Probst, Robert: "The Human Performer in the Machine-related Office," *Environment/Planning and Design,* January/February 1970.

Probst, Robert: *The Office, a Facility Based on Change,* The Business Press, Elmhurst, Illinois, 1968.

Project 71, Mercedes-Benz of North America, Fort Lee, New Jersey, March 1970.

Read, W. H.: "Upward Communications in Industrial Hierarchies," *Human Relations,* no. 15, 1962.

A Report of the ODCASO Office Landscape Furnishings and Equipment, U.S. Department of Labor and General Services Administration, Washington, D.C., 1969.

Riland, Lane H., and Joan R. Kurtz: *Employee Reactions to a Landscape Office Environment,* Eastman Kodak Company, Rochester, New York, November 1968.

Riland, Lane H.: *Resurvey of Employee Reactions to the Landscape Environment One Year after Initial Occupation,* Eastman Kodak Company, Rochester, New York, March 1970.

Simon, Herbert A.: "The Architecture of Complexity," *Kommunikation,* vol. 3, no. 2, 1967.

Smith, Peter B.: "Relations between Managers and Their Associates," *Administrative Science Quarterly,* vol. 14, no. 3, September 1969.

Stephenson, B.: *The Study of Behavior,* University of Chicago Press, Chicago, 1953.

Trebesch, Karsten, and Dieter Jaeger: "An Analysis of the Significance and Distribution of Status Symbols in Bureaucratic Organizations," *Kommunikation,* vol. 3, no. 4, 1971.

Index

Index

T.C.